Interface Design

Creating Interactions that Drive Successful Product Adoption

Couche, Guillaume
Shackleton, Richard
Iliffe, Samuel

Interface Design: Creating Interactions that Drive Successful Product
Adoption

BIS Publishers
Borneostraat 80-A
1094 CP Amsterdam
The Netherlands

T +31 (0)20 515 02 30
bis@bispublishers.com
www.bispublishers.com

ISBN: 978-90-636-9710-5

Interface Design

Creating Interactions that Drive Successful Product Adoption

Guillaume Couche
Richard Shackleton
Samuel Iliffe

BISPUBLISHERS

Contents

Introduction

Throughout much of our history, machines were specialised, scarce and often shared amongst large groups of humans. Logically, their design was mostly results-oriented, intended to benefit the group rather than the individual. Consider a Roman catapult or a wood lathe — in both cases it is unlikely that anyone initially thought about 'user experience' during their construction. This remained mostly true until the emergence of machines such as the automobile and, later, the personal computer, in the twentieth century. Today, machines are ubiquitous, versatile and largely personalised. In fact, between cars, computers, home appliances, phones and other connected devices, we are surrounded by machines and spend most of our time interacting with one kind or another. This change of purpose has had significant consequences on machine design, with questions that sometimes revolve exclusively around the quality of user experience. Yet, if this was enabled by technological evolution, it also came from a change in the way we perceive a core element of machines: the interface.

For a long time, interfaces and their constituent inputs were functional parts of machines. Typically, a gear-shifting lever would act as a physical bridge between the hand of a driver and a vehicle's gearbox. With the invention of electricity came mechanical decoupling between the interface and the actual mechanism. However, the interface remained a functional part of the machine. A music amplifier knob, for instance, allowed for increasing or decreasing the volume of music by modifying the resistance inside the machine's electrical circuit. This changed with the introduction of advanced electronics and computing, as it enabled the use of interface inputs that would not have to be integrated as a functional part of the machine itself. Previously selected based on specific mechanical or electrical properties, interface inputs like knobs could now be considered a means to gather user instructions in the form of an electrical signal, later to be processed electronically or digitally. The processed instruction could be used to drive various machine functionalities, opening up a large number of design possibilities — from input selection, to programming their behaviour.

Interestingly, the combination of virtually infinite options, and an interface independent from the machine itself, meant that interface design could suddenly be considered separately, sometimes secondarily. As a consequence, while new, innovative machines appeared, they remained only usable by a narrow typology of users. A typical example is the early computer that could be operated solely through command lines, requiring the learning of specific instructions and their syntax. Inventors like Douglas Engelbart saw how crucial it would become for humans to be able to use machines effectively. Their research led to the creation of a new design field — *interaction design* — and inspired visionary entrepreneurs such as Steve Jobs. In many ways, Apple's success can be seen as the history of a company that understood, earlier than its competitors, the importance of focusing primarily on interface design in order to build universally appealing machines.

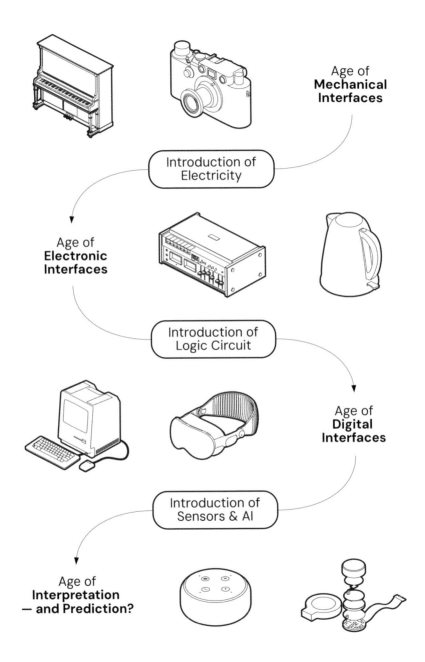

Age of **Mechanical Interfaces**

Introduction of Electricity

Age of **Electronic Interfaces**

Introduction of Logic Circuit

Age of **Digital Interfaces**

Introduction of Sensors & AI

Age of **Interpretation — and Prediction?**

Today, interfaces are the keystone of every single product and service that sees the light of day. There are dozens of job titles that correspond to positions whose responsibilities are directly, or indirectly, related to interface design. While segmenting roles in large organisations is important to delineate responsibilities, it also establishes boundaries. Consequently, we see design practices that develop their own jargon and literature, sometimes overlooking shared origins and creative opportunities that arise from the cross-pollination of ideas.

Interfaces are rapidly evolving, and we might be on the verge of witnessing another major paradigm shift: modern sensors and artificial intelligence allow for interpreting, and even predicting, the user's intention without any active interaction. Beyond the complexity this adds to navigating the potential design opportunities, it also raises ethical and philosophical questions about the impact these changes might have on human agency and our ability to interact with one another.

With this book, we aim to provide the widest lens for thinking about machines and their interfaces for all designers, product managers, engineers, hobbyists and creatives alike, whether one's experience and interests lie in industrial and product design, spatial computing and virtual reality, user interface (UI) and user experience (UX), interaction and installation design, or software and application development.

Authors' note: for simplicity, and to avoid repetition, in the following chapters we describe the general case — that is, mostly hand or finger actuation. However, most concepts and principles can be implemented for any type of body actuation (hand, foot, elbow, eye). Other concepts (e.g. language-based interaction) do not rely on body motion at all. While we considered rating these concepts based on an 'accessibility' criterion, establishing absolute terms proves challenging as it depends on the specific needs of the individual, applications and final design. Given the extensive overview of the interface landscape, we believe this book can be used as a helpful tool to invent solutions and find alternatives to make interfaces more accessible. Ultimately, it comes down to one simple question when working on a new design: does it also work for people who are not like me?

'Apple's success can be seen as the history of a company that understood, earlier than its competitors, the importance of focusing primarily on interface design in order to build universally appealing machines.'

1/ Definitions

In this chapter, we provide an overview and reference base for specific and recurring concepts used throughout the book. While the definitions given closely align with the primary usage in the English language, we often restrict the meaning of specific terms for the purpose of disambiguation. Conversely, we occasionally provide widely recognised definitions to insist on the wider lens we apply to them. The presentation is primarily organised by association.

Machine

We consider the term 'machine' in its widest meaning, to designate any object, physical or virtual, with interaction capabilities. Typical machines we use in our daily life include cars, smartphones, speakers, cameras and kitchen appliances.

Computer: while it has become commonplace to consider nearly every machine as a computer, for clarity, we reserve this term specifically for personal computers, tablets and smartphones.

Interaction

A 'human–machine interaction', or simply an 'interaction', is a set of actions performed alternatively by a human and a machine, with multiple potential outcomes. Interactions are sometimes metaphorically described as the dialogue between the human and the machine. Pressing a sequence of buttons on a phone keypad *is* an interaction. Using a mouse to create digital content on a computer *is* an interaction. Exchanging with a chatbot to access one's bank accounts *is* an interaction. While some hold the view that the term 'interaction' can only be used when the outcome cannot be predicted by a simple action–reaction mechanism, the distinction is becoming increasingly hard to make when machines are all becoming intelligent. Today, there is, in practice, no base unit for what is deemed an 'interaction'. For instance driving a car, with all that entails, and turning the wheel can both be considered interactions, even if the former contains the latter.

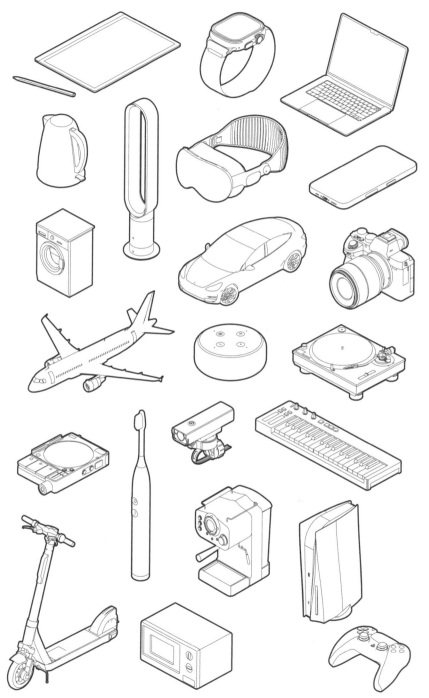

Active interaction: an active interaction is the default interaction, and this is what people usually refer to when they speak of 'interactions'. It always follows a conscious decision from the user to engage with the machine. If the interaction is not active, we speak of 'passive' interaction.

Passive interaction: contrary to an active interaction, where the user *makes* a decision to engage with a machine, a passive interaction can happen without this intention. For instance, a portable speaker might be designed to play music when someone comes within a specified detection range. Whether or not this person is the primary user, i.e. the user who installed the device, a conscious decision may not have been made for the interaction to happen, *at the moment it happens*. Hence, this is a *passive* interaction. It is worth noting that passive interactions can go beyond automations and routines that would have been set up by a human. For instance, the device described here might use artificial intelligence to perform actions such as changing the music based on the assumed mood of the user.

Routine: usually set up by the user, a routine is a predefined procedure allowing for automating the actions performed by a machine based on data collected by a sensor, or a set of sensors. A typical home automation routine is to switch on the heating when the temperature drops below a certain level.

Interface

An ensemble of inputs and feedback systems that allow for interaction with a machine.

Physical interface: sometimes referred to as a 'human-machine interface', a physical interface is made of hardware inputs such as physical buttons, knobs, sliders, or sensors. A computer keyboard is an example of physical interface.

Graphical user interface: a graphical user interface (GUI) is an interface made of software inputs such as virtual buttons, knobs and sliders, represented to the user by means of a display or headset (e.g. spatial computing). A smartphone menu is an example of a graphical user interface. User experience (UX) and user interface (UI) designers specialise, amongst other things, in the design of graphical user interfaces.

Primary interface: a graphical user interface always requires a physical interface to act as an entry point for the user to interact with it. Typically, operating a smartphone menu (graphical user interface) requires touch interactions on the device's touch screen (physical interface). When the distinction needs to be made, we speak of 'primary interface' for the physical one.

Input

An input is both the entry point and mechanism by which a human can interact with a machine. See Chapter 2 for more details and a list of the existing families of inputs.

Component: throughout the book, the term 'input' is used to describe general concepts and, sometimes, their implementation. We speak of 'hardware component' or just 'component' when we refer to the underlying technology of a given input.

Maintained: an input is described as 'maintained' when it keeps returning the last state, or value, it has been set to by the user. The opposite of 'maintained' is 'momentary'.

Momentary: an input is deemed 'momentary' if it always returns its default state, or value, when not in operation. The opposite of 'momentary' is 'maintained'.

Signal: when an input returns continuous values we speak of 'signal'. For inputs with set boundaries, the signal can be represented as a percentage of the full input range. Typically, the signal of a slider could be anything between 0% and 100%.

States: when an input returns discrete values we speak of 'states'. Typically, a button input will return 1 when pressed and 0 when not. States are often characterised using words rather than values to avoid ambiguity. In the previous example, 1 would be referred to as 'ON' or 'ACTIVE' and 0 as 'OFF' or 'INACTIVE'.

Spatial computing

Spatial computing is an umbrella concept that covers all the computing interactions happening outside of the boundaries imposed by traditional computers and flat graphical user interfaces. We use it specifically when it involves immersive three-dimensional (3D) technologies such as virtual reality (VR), augmented reality (AR), mixed reality (MR) and spatial audio.

Kinaesthetic

We use the term 'kinaesthetic' when a specific concept relates to the user's awareness of the position and movement of their body, or parts of their body. 'Kinaesthetic memory', for instance, is a central mechanism through which humans learn to play an instrument, while 'kinaesthetic mapping' describes our ability to intuitively find our way on an interface. An input will be described as providing more or less 'kinaesthetic feedback' depending on how much it lets the user feel the movements necessary to operate it (see Chapter 3 for more details).

'Interactions are sometimes metaphorically described as the dialogue between the human and the machine.'

2/ Input Concepts

The concepts described in this section are theoretical definitions of the different inputs that can be used to create an interface. These are not to be confused with actual hardware components. In fact, a given input concept might entail different physical realities, each relying on the use of distinctive components. Conversely, one same component can be used as the foundation brick for various input concepts. For instance, a joystick, a trigger and a knob are all built with the same hardware component: a rotary potentiometer (two in the case of the joystick – one for the vertical direction and one for the horizontal direction). Yet, and as we shall see, a joystick, a trigger and a knob are *different* input concepts, each with entirely distinct sets of properties.

For each concept, we provide defining characteristics, some examples of real-life implementations and variations. We also highlight the modalities of interaction — the mechanisms by which the user can change the value or state of the input as described in the following list:

- **Moving:** the user has to translate the moving part of the input along two or more axes.

- **None:** the user is not supposed to engage in any form of active interaction (although passive interactions are the goal).

- **Pressing**: the user has to exercise pressure on the input.

- **Sliding:** the user has to translate the moving part of the input along one axis.

- **Speaking:** the user has to voice out an instruction using predefined commands, or engage in a conversation.

- **Squeezing:** the user has to exercise pressure on the input, usually by compressing it between their palm and index finger.

- **Tapping:** the user has to actuate the input by using velocity rather than pure pressure.

- **Touch-moving:** the user has to translate their fingers, or a stylus, on the surface of the input.

- **Track-moving:** the user has to translate and/or rotate the tracked part of a handheld device or any part of their body, in two dimensions (2D) or three dimensions (3D), anywhere in the areas of their space covered by the tracking sensors of the input.

- **Turning:** the user has to rotate the moving part of the input.

- **Typing:** the user has to press keys in order to form commands, or engage in a conversation.

Potentiometer: Rotary or linear, a potentiometer is a manually adjustable resistor. While traditional applications included changing the volume of a radio or dimming lights it is now commonly used to control an adjustable variable through a rotary or linear motion.

Where applicable, we provide a radar chart to allow for comparison across 7 criteria:

- **Motor control:** *how easy is the input to use without training or special skills?* Typically, knobs and sliders are easy to operate and set to a specific value, irrespective of the user's abilities and training. On the opposite end of the spectrum, finding the right amount of force to apply to a pressure button can be hard, even after some practice.

- **Range:** *how many values or states does the input allow for reaching?* A button is typically the least range here, offering two states by default. A bounded knob will have much more range, with hundreds of possibilities, while an infinite knob will accommodate for an infinity of values.

- **Frequency:** *does the input allow for repeating multiple operations at a high frequency?* Momentary inputs, such as the ones that can be found on a video game controller (e.g. buttons and triggers) have high frequency. Conversely, maintained inputs such as bounded knobs and sliders have low frequency.

- **Expressiveness:** *is the input capable of capturing subtle changes or expression?* Input concepts used for music (trigger keys on keyboards, pressure buttons on drum pads and spatial tracking) are considered more expressive. Unsurprisingly, discrete state inputs, such as buttons and switches, are less expressive.

- **Feedback:** *is the input naturally capable of providing feedback on progress towards the desired value or state?* Bounded knobs and sliders are easy to read both visually and by touching them whereas touch surfaces always remain visually and physically the same.

- **Versatility:** *does the input allow for controlling a complex output such as a 2D or 3D position?* Again, discrete state inputs such as buttons and switches score the lowest here, while touch surfaces and tracking score the highest.

- **Stability:** *does the input allow for holding a state or value easily for a chosen amount of time or permanently?* While buttons offer the highest level of stability, pressure buttons offer the lowest as maintaining pressure at a certain level is difficult whatever the skill set of the user.

While reading these charts, one should keep in mind they cover the median case of each input concept theoretically, and provide a general comparison only. In practice, how they perform along each criterion may vary depending on the physical implementation and, in some cases, software or firmware behaviour. We will examine this in Chapter 3 and Chapter 4 respectively.

Button

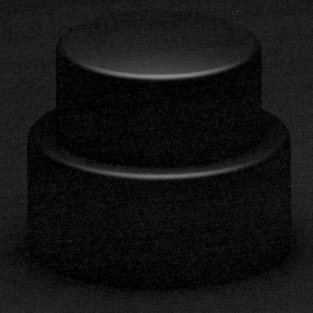

Momentary input with two discrete states: 'active' when pressed, or 'inactive' when not.

Modality of interaction: *pressing*

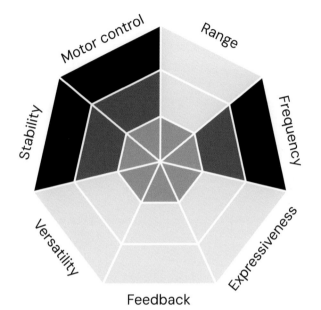

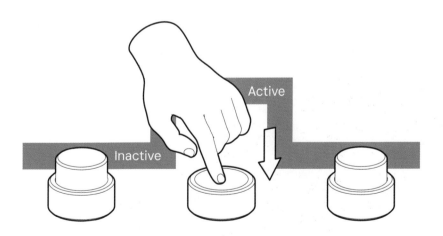

Implementations and variations

Traditionally, buttons require the user to press a moving part, providing a tangible impression of their activation, sometimes with a 'click'.

More and more often, mechanical buttons are replaced by non-moving touch buttons, integrated in a larger surface. This can facilitate easy cleaning (e.g. kitchen appliances) and usually comes with the addition of sound feedback when pressed, however losing the physicality of the button can leave an unsatisfying experience.

Some buttons may have an extra intermediate state which the user can feel thanks to the inclusion of a notch. Typically, the shutter button on a digital camera will allow this to activate focusing before snapping a picture. This can require more subtle motor control from the user.

Left: Sony A6400 camera (2019), a calculator, a set of physical buttons and a touch button

Pressure button

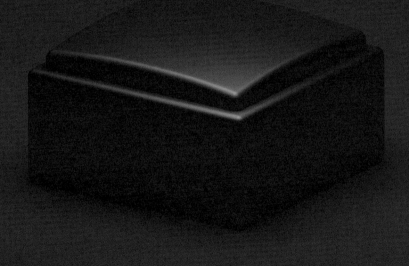

Momentary input that provides a continuous signal reflecting how much pressure is exercised on it by the user.

Modality of interaction: *pressing* or *tapping*

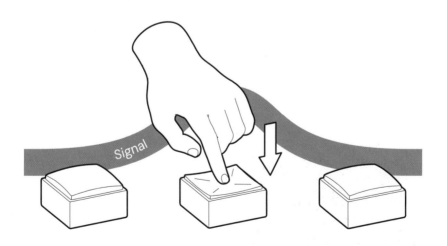

Implementations and variations

Pressure buttons usually do not rely on the use of a moving part to establish the amount of pressure applied to them. As a consequence, they can be difficult to operate, and painful at times, especially when the user does not know how much pressure to apply in order to obtain the desired effect. This can be mitigated by adding a flexible membrane as a top layer, providing a softer touch and a tangible impression of the pressure being applied as it deforms. Key pads and drum pads are usually made of a rubbery material so as they can be pressed delicately or tapped upon in a rhythm (with natural bounce).

Alternatively, haptic feedback (see Chapter 3) can be used to provide the illusion that the pressure button is moving or 'clicking', as featured on the now discontinued '3D Touch' on Apple's iPhones and 'Force Touch' on Apple trackpads (as we will see later, these are not just pressure buttons but combined inputs).

Left (top to bottom): Apple iPhone 6S (2015), Novation Launchpad Mini MkII music controller (2015), Akai MPC500 drum machine (2008)

Trigger

Momentary input that provides a continuous signal corresponding to the travel of its moving part, which returns to the default position when released.

Modality of interaction: *pressing* or *squeezing*

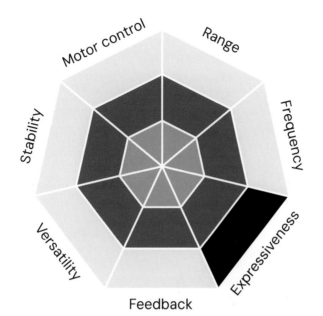

Motor control Range

Stability Frequency

Versatility Expressiveness

Feedback

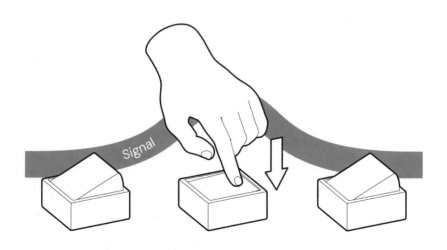

Signal

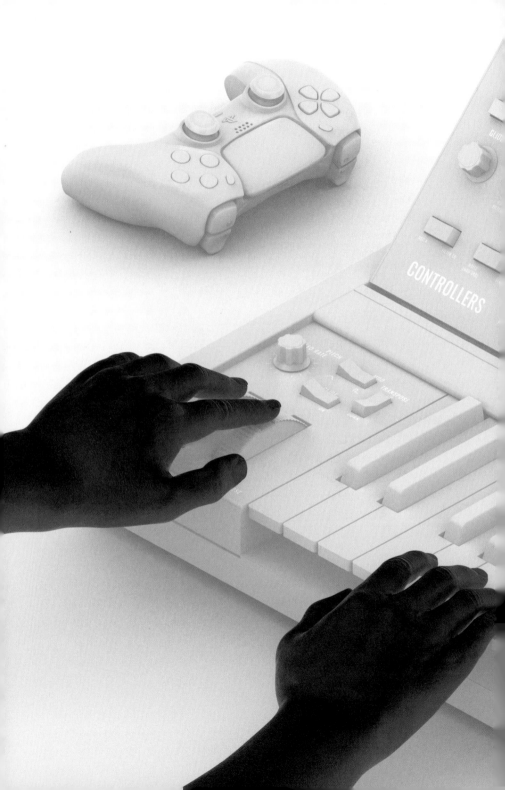

Implementations and variations

Triggers are usually in the form of a button shaped to be pressed by the index finger while the other fingers hold the whole interface. This particular form factor is what enables adequate motor control, allowing the user to navigate between different levels of squeezing, easily and intuitively.

Today, triggers can be found on most video game controllers with applications that range from the expected first-person shooters to car and plane simulation. In the latter case, triggers are often used to emulate foot pedals, which can themselves be added to the extended trigger family.

Finally, the keys and modulation wheels found on most piano keyboards and synthesisers are triggers. Measuring travel is enough to calculate the velocity of a key pressed by a musician in order to modulate the emitted sound and 'add expression to it'. However, some designs combine a trigger and a pressure button in order for the key to remain expressive *after it has been struck,* and while it is being held down. This architecture is commonly referred to as 'aftertouch'.

Left (top to bottom): Playstation 5 gamepad (2020), Behringer Poly D analogue synthesiser (2019)

Switch

Maintained input with two, or more, discrete states.

Modality of interaction: *pressing, turning* or *sliding*
depending on the form factor

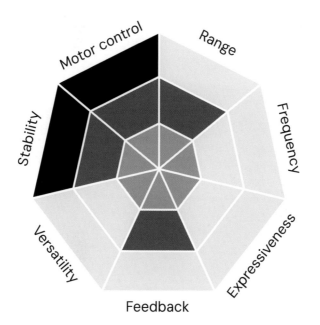

Motor control
Range
Frequency
Stability
Expressiveness
Versatility
Feedback

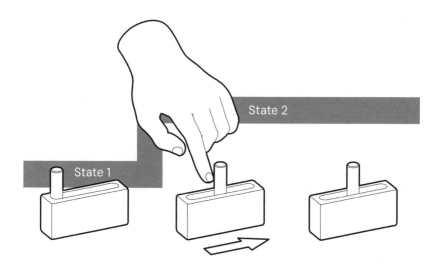

State 2

State 1

39

Implementations and variations

Switches can be in the form factor of a button, a knob, a toggle, or a slider. Their typical use is for turning machines or functionalities 'ON' and 'OFF'. They can also be used to switch between usage modes (e.g. camera modes).

Ideally, the design of a switch should provide visual and tactile feedback on its current state, so the user does not need to operate it to find out which state is set and which other states are available.

This is not always possible however, especially when instead of a switch, another input is modified to behave like one, as we will see in Chapter 4. The modern bicycle light is a common example, where a simple button input is used as a multiple state switch, requiring multiple presses to cycle through states, a sometimes frustrating trial and error approach from the user to find the desired lighting mode.

Left: Different types of switches and a switch-controlled table fan

Bounded knob

Maintained input that provides a continuous signal corresponding to the rotation of its moving part between two boundaries.

Modality of interaction: *turning*

Motor control

Range

Frequency

Expressiveness

Feedback

Versatility

Stability

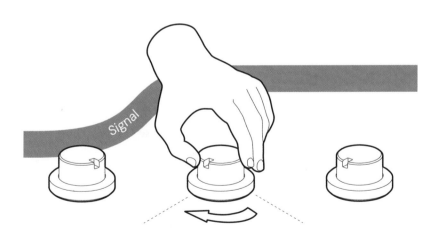

Signal

43

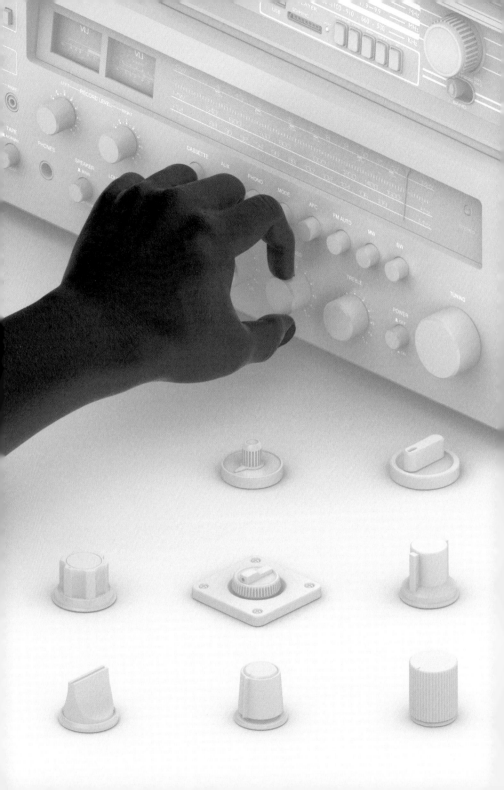

Implementations and variations

Bounded knobs are often designed to offer an indication of their current value at a glance. They can be bigger or smaller, and operated with all five fingers, just two or even one.

Some have a detent at mid-rotation (e.g. a stereo left/right balance knob on a music amplifier) or many detents to allow for selecting many discrete values (e.g. the exposure compensation wheel on a camera).

Detent: A small mechanism to help hold a position or rotation and prevent undesired movement of the moving part of the input.

Left: *Funai Stereo Cassette player (1971) and various bounded knob designs*

Infinite knob

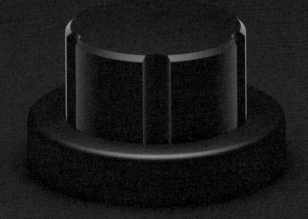

Maintained input that provides a continuous signal corresponding to the rotation of its moving part without boundaries.

Modality of interaction: *turning*

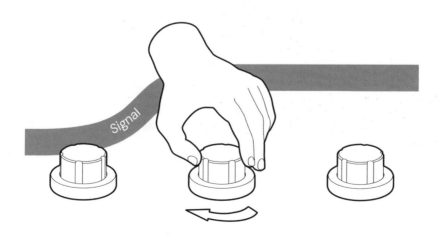

47

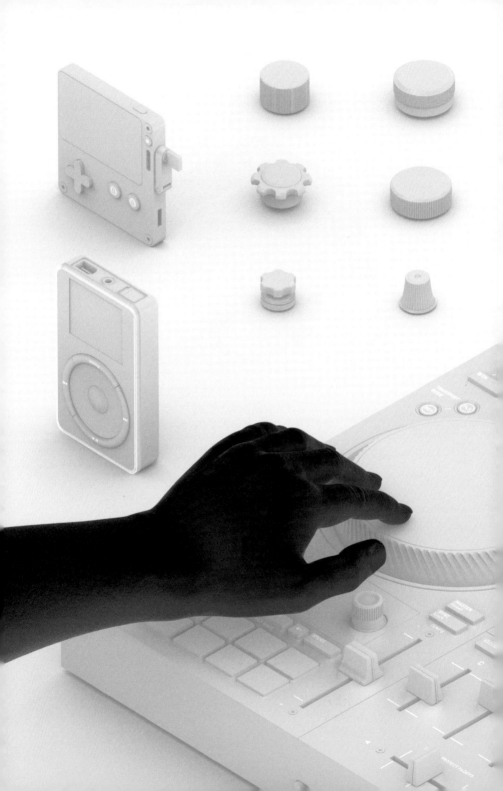

Implementations and variations

Like bounded knobs, infinite knobs can be bigger or smaller and operated with all five fingers, just two or even one.

Unlike bounded knobs, infinite knobs do not have a start or end rotation. Hence, they cannot have any marking that would provide feedback on the current value. To compensate for that, a reconfigurable value display or circular display (e.g. a ring of LED lights) is often added to provide visual feedback.

Infinite knobs can also have detents for added tactile feedback when rotated or, as with bounded knobs, for controlling discrete values where clear steps help the interaction. High-end knobs can use motors to simulate mechanical detents, with the advantage of allowing adjustable granularity.

Sometimes, infinite knobs take the form of a crank wheel allowing for uninterrupted spinning.

Left (top to bottom): *Panic Playdate video game console (2022), Apple iPod music player (2001), Native Instruments Traktor Kontrol S4 MKIII DJ decks (2018)*

Slider

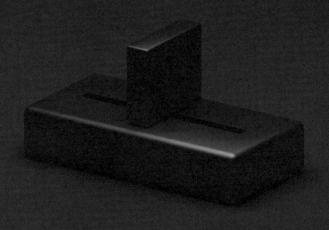

Maintained input that provides a continuous signal corresponding to the translation of its moving part between two boundaries.

Modality of interaction: *sliding*

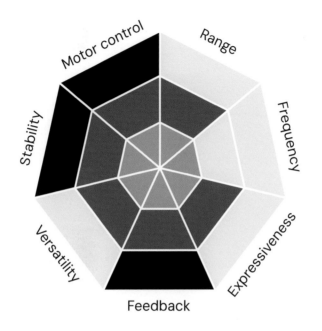

Motor control

Range

Frequency

Expressiveness

Feedback

Versatility

Stability

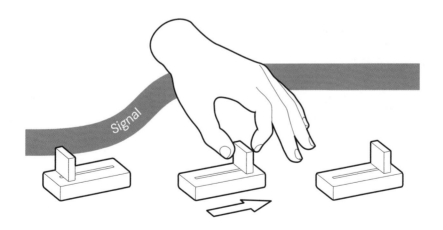

Signal

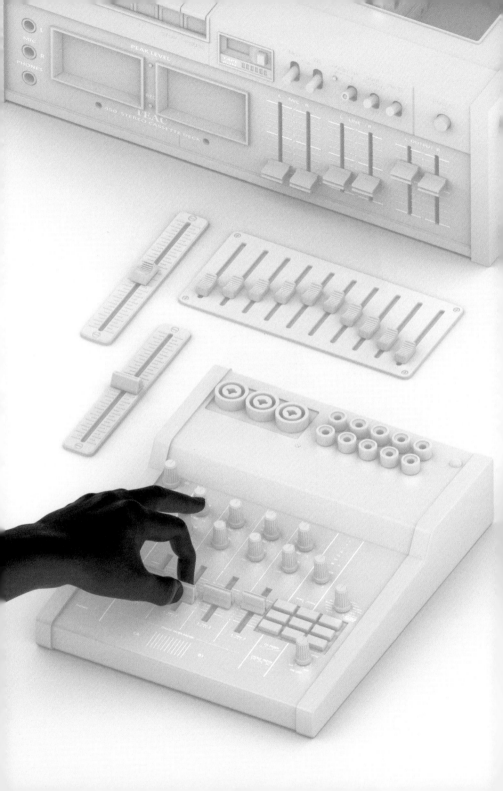

Implementations and variations

Sliders exist in a variety of lengths. They naturally provide a high level of mapping, making them ideally suited for quick visualisation of a large number of inputs (e.g. audio levels on a mixing table).

Sliders can feature a detent at mid-course to help the user with zeroing a parameter, or a series of detents to help feel the progression.

High-end interfaces sometimes feature motorised sliders that can reposition themselves automatically, either occasionally, to match a specific configuration, or dynamically, to replay parameter automations. Motors can also be used to simulate mechanical detents, with the advantage of allowing for adjustable granularity.

Left (top to bottom): Teac 450 Stereo Cassette Deck player (1972), six tracks analogue mixing console (unknown manufacturer)

Joystick

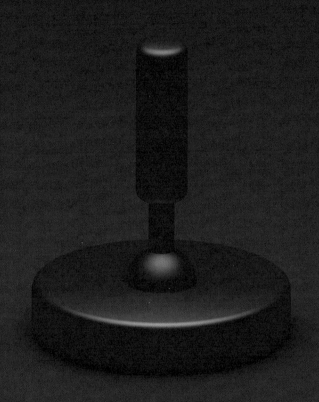

Momentary or maintained input that provides two
continuous signals corresponding to the travel of its
moving part along two axes, each constrained by two
boundaries. If momentary, the moving part returns to
its default position when released.

Modality of interaction: *moving*

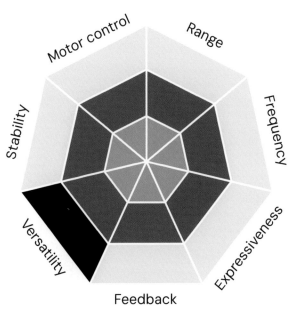

Motor control

Range

Frequency

Stability

Expressiveness

Versatility

Feedback

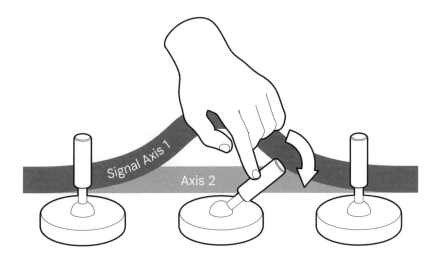

Signal Axis 1

Axis 2

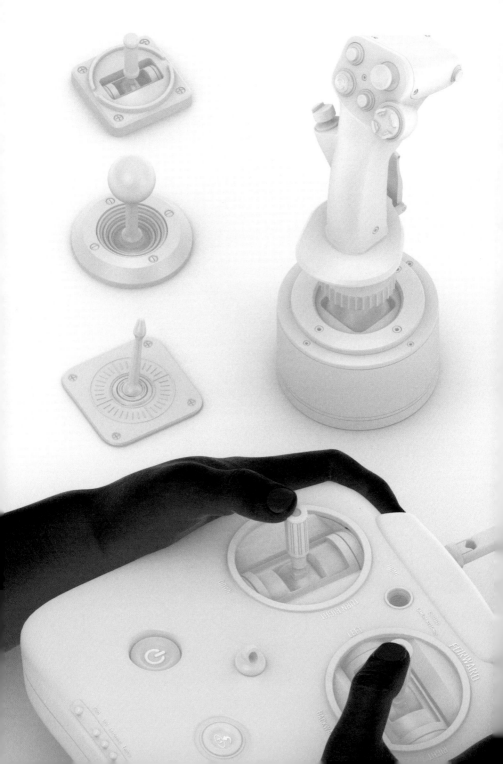

Implementations and variations

There are different sizes and designs of joysticks allowing them to be operated with the whole hand, two fingers or just the thumb. While hand joysticks are commonly associated with planes and helicopters because of their stable nature, smaller joysticks are typical of game controllers and remote controls for model planes, where their compact size helps with reactivity (see the Chapter 3 for more information on why large planes need *stability* and small ones *reactivity*).

Contrary to the more common momentary joysticks, *maintained* joysticks have no spring mechanism to make the moving part return to its default position when released. They, too, can be found on remote controls for model planes or drones, some synthesisers and stage lighting control consoles.

Left (top to bottom right): *Aircraft joystick (unknown manufacturer), Drone controller (unknown manufacturer)*

Rolling

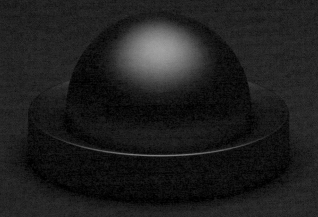

Maintained input that provides two continuous signals corresponding to the travel of its moving part along two axes without boundaries.

Modality of interaction: *moving*

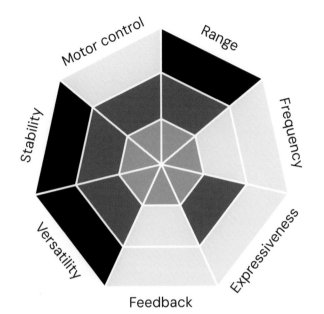

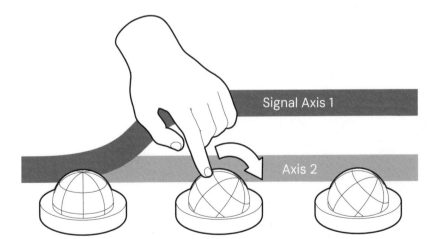

Implementations and variations

Ubiquitous with the personal computer, mice remain the weapon of choice when it comes to precise desktop computer work. They can be designed to be ergonomic or sleek and minimalistic, wired or wireless; the dust magnets using a soft rolling ball are a thing of the past.

Although modern mice use direct optical tracking to know where they are and laptop manufacturers have long opted for trackpads, the rolling ball has not entirely disappeared. Trackballs can be found on the top of ergonomic mice, on medical equipment and on colour grading interfaces. They work especially well in this latter case where three trackballs can be used to adjust multiple parameters simultaneously.

Left (top to bottom): Apple Macintosh with its Macintosh Mouse (1984), Tangent Wave CP300 colour grading surface (2009)

Touch surface

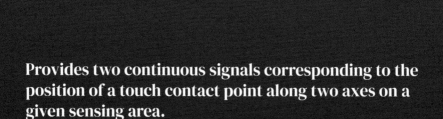

Provides two continuous signals corresponding to the position of a touch contact point along two axes on a given sensing area.

Modality of interaction: *touch-moving*

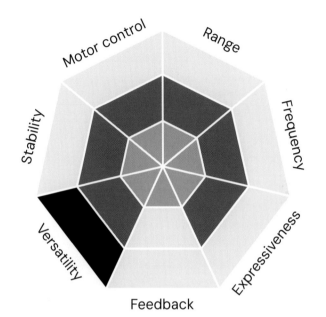

Motor control

Range

Frequency

Stability

Expressiveness

Versatility

Feedback

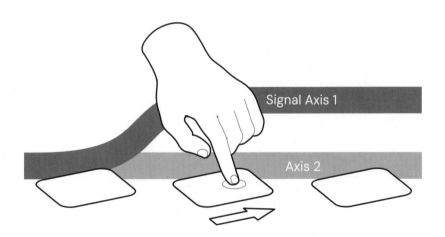

Signal Axis 1

Axis 2

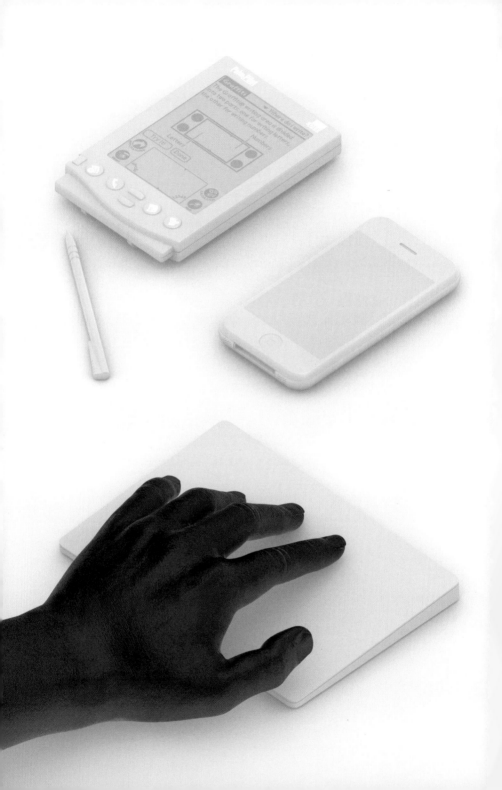

Implementations and variations

Touch surfaces have become one of the dominant forms of input with the rise of smartphones, laptop computers, and smart watches. A trackpad is a touch surface; a touch screen is a touch surface combined with a display. Depending on designs and implementations, they can be used directly with fingers, or with a stylus.

Besides their pointing ability, touch surfaces can also be programmed to detect gestures. Increasingly, they are often combined with a haptic feedback system to give the illusion of clicking without there being moving parts.

Less common, one-dimensional touch surfaces exist in ribbon or wheel form factors.

***Left (top to bottom):** Palm Pilot personal digital assistant (1996), Apple iPhone (2007), Apple Magic Trackpad 3 (2021)*

Tracking

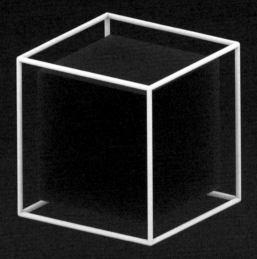

Provides continuous signals corresponding to the position, rotation or specific pose in place of a held device or any part of the human body.

Modality of interaction: *track-moving*

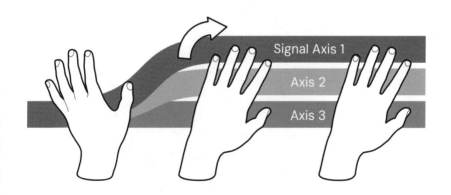

Implementations and variations

Popularised in the mid 2000s by the Nintendo Wii and the Microsoft Xbox Kinect, tracking allows for using body motion and gestures to interact with a machine, typically to manipulate virtual content visualised on a monitor or through a head-mounted display. The tracked entities can be part of the human body — usually the hands — or a proxy object (e.g. a controller), the latter allowing for bundling tracking with other input concepts such as buttons, triggers and trackpads.

There are various technologies such as cameras, inertial sensors and radar (e.g. Google Soli) that can be used for tracking. When it relies on the continuous analysis of one or more camera feeds, it can raise privacy concerns for the user.

Left (top to bottom): Nintendo Wii Remote game controller (2006), Microsoft Kinect motion sensing input device (2010)

Language

Provides a way to perform various tasks from simple to complex, based on human or other defined language.

Modality of interaction: *Speaking* or *typing*

Implementations and variations

As an input concept, language has long relied on typing instructions in command lines or code, usually based on the English language. After being replaced by graphical user interfaces for the most common tasks, it is coming back in the form of voice assistants powered by artificial intelligence. Users can now speak out when they need something, in their own language, and without having to learn specific machine terminology.

Voice assistants might feature a barrier, or 'invocation mechanism' to avoid unintended interactions and deflect privacy concerns. The idea is to continuously process short loops of audio with the sole aim of detecting a trigger word. Once it has been detected, feedback is given to the user (e.g. the voice assistant speaks back) and the conversation starts. Only then does full audio processing take place, stopping when the conversation stops, until the next 'invocation'.

Left (top to bottom): Amazon Echo smart speaker (2014), Keychron K8 wireless mechanical keyboard (2020)

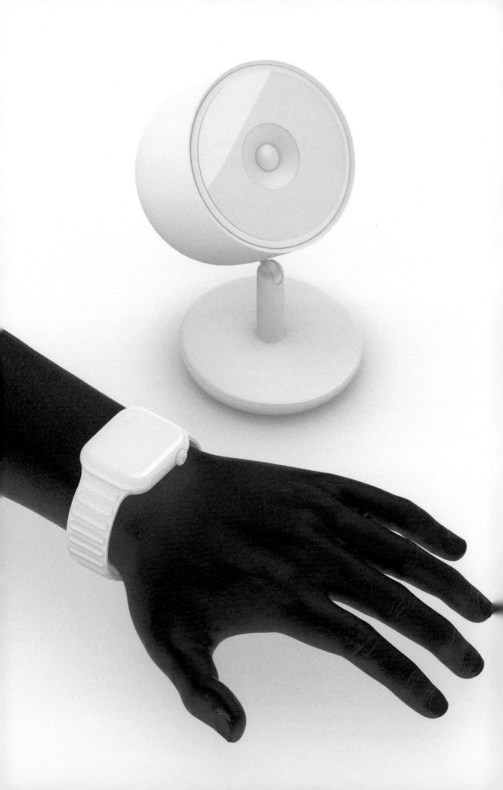

Sensor

Provides data to be treated by algorithms or artificial intelligence in order to adjust the machine's response.

Modality of interaction: *Usually none (passive)*

Implementations and variations

Whether as standalone devices or as part of larger interfaces, the use of sensors is on the rise in interaction design. Common examples include automation allowing for the adjustment of light, temperature or music volume based on routines created by the user. However, the use of artificial intelligence opens the door to far more complex forms of automation when the logic may be based on large sets of data and predictive algorithms.

Concepts such as implantable brain-computer interfaces, whose aim is to detect intentions at the neuronal level, arguably belong to a separate typology of inputs. They are closer to tracking, since they may accommodate for a form of active interaction. In practice, this will depend, for each specific implementation, on how intentions are inferred, and on the exact role of predictive algorithms in that process.

Left (top to bottom): Google Nest Cam IQ indoor camera (2017), Apple Watch Series 7 with its movement and health tracking sensors (2021)

Virtual inputs

Any of the previously discussed input concepts, simulated in software and represented in 2D via a monitor screen, or 3D through a head-mounted display (such as a mixed reality headset).

Modality of interaction: *Depends on the modality of interaction of the primary (physical) interface and rules established in software. For instance, moving the mouse (physical) might translate into rotating a virtual knob.*

Implementations and variations

Virtual inputs on flat screens, buttons, switches, and sliders are by far the most common. Menus — specifically drop-down menus — advantageously replace multi-state switches. As for 2D inputs, they usually have a rectangular or circular shape with a touch-surface behaviour (e.g. a colour wheel).

Spatial graphical user interfaces build on users' habits with flat ones and can make use of the extra dimension to various ends: turning flat inputs into 3D inputs for added functionality or style reasons, designing inputs that fully emulate physical ones, or just increasing the 'interface real estate'.

3/ Physical Design

Designing objects, whether consumer goods, furniture or even buildings, is traditionally an all-encompassing process, where a balance has to be found between various attributes such as usability, aesthetics, cost, manufacturability and ergonomics, to name the most common.

While this remains true with machines, the unfathomable diversity of potential uses — which expands with technological progress — brings an odd question into the equation: *how does it do what?* Increasingly, designing interactions is trying to find answers to this double interrogation.

An interaction is an abstract concept and there is only so much control one can have on how people will behave when confronted with a machine. This is why interaction design seeks to form hypotheses through the building and testing of functional prototypes. To that end, it should be noted that, beyond the choice of the input concept itself, the way it is designed — physically — will have a tremendous impact on how it performs for the intended interaction.

This chapter starts with five sections that correspond to the questions designers should consider for each input of a given interface:

- How should it be handled?
- How much should it travel?
- How firm should it be?
- How much inertia should it have?
- How does it provide feedback?

These are followed by a practical guide and a section dedicated to graphical user interfaces.

We speak of 'physical' design because most of the principles we cover in this chapter derive directly from fundamental laws of physics and human anatomy. This is not to say that it solely concerns physical interfaces. In fact, even graphical user interfaces displayed on flat screens are designed with physical constraints in mind. For instance, the design of a button, whether it is physical or a virtual, has to take into account the size of a fingertip. Moreover, the rise of spatial computing implies virtual designs that are increasingly concerned with real world scale and physically plausible mechanisms.

This form of mechanical mimicry has resonances with skeuomorphism, and a similar purpose. Indeed, when a digital interface behaves in a physically sound way, it makes it more intuitive to the human brain which, in turn, can open the door to massively successful interactions. 'Inertial scrolling', popularised by Apple with the first iPhone in 2007 is still, almost two decades later, the main navigation interaction for smartphones, tablets and laptops. Finally, it is precisely the seamless interplay between the design of their physical and graphical user interfaces that makes the most iconic products of the last decades so extraordinarily popular, and great to use.

'how does it do what? Increasingly, designing interactions is trying to find answers to this double interrogation.'

Skeuomorphism: A skeuomorph is an object that features decorative attributes reminiscent of the structure of the object it derives from. Fake sculpted nails at the top of Greek temples that mimic the structure of anterior wooden temples are examples of skeuomorphs. Skeuomorphism is the action of using skeuomorphs in art or design. While some see skeuomorphism as purely ornamental, it has been widely used in user interface (UI) design to help new users guess functionality by making virtual inputs look similar to known physical ones.

Handling

How is it supposed to be handled?

This is the first question that should come to mind when designing an interface. Naturally, it implies other questions: is it intended for adults or children? Can it be used by people with different abilities? Is it actuated with the hand? with a finger? with a foot? How often, how quickly, and what is the accuracy of the end result?

Beyond an understanding of the target audience and their desired goal, answering these questions requires understanding about how handling affects the whole interaction choreography.

The way an input is handled is largely determined by the:

- scale of the input
- orientation of the input
- layout of the interface
- materials and surface of the input.

Handling: scale

The scale of an input is one of the first factors that determines which part of our body we will use to actuate it. When confronted with small buttons and knobs, we typically use the tips of our fingers. Faced with larger ones and without the need for any other noticeable change in the design we will use a full hand.

'each chain of joints ... is capable of unique motions with a unique range of strength.'

By doing so, we change the configuration of the body joints in use which, in turn, changes our perception of the properties of the input. For instance, we might find one input more suitable for precise but slow control, and the other one best for fast but less accurate operations, even if the underlying hardware components are strictly the same and nothing in their design can suggest different abilities. This difference in perception is explained by the fact that each chain of joints, or kinetic chain, that our body can form, is capable of unique motions with a unique range of strength.

Consider a hand joystick and a thumb joystick with the exact same hardware components, handle aside.

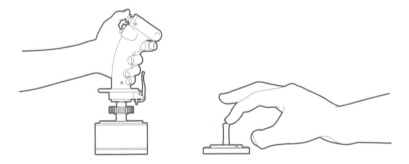

Because of the way it is to be handled, the hand joystick requires movements from all of the arm joints to be operated. In addition, and due to the scale of these joints, these movements have to be of high amplitude for a noticeable change to happen.

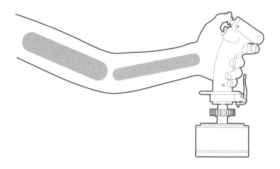

This makes holding a certain position relatively easy, and undesired changes or accidents less likely. On the flip side, a hand joystick will not be quick or comfortable enough for repeated changes.

Conversely, the thumb joystick only requires movement of the finger joints. Due to the scale of these joints and the way the human body works, fast operations and repetitions become relatively easy to achieve while precision and the ability to hold specific positions are limited.

This is why, despite the many radical changes that have affected the way planes are designed, hand joysticks are still the input of choice when it comes to flying them. Interestingly, however, remotely controlled model planes are usually flown using a thumb joystick. While this is certainly explained in part by the fact that model plane control interfaces have to be small enough to be carried easily, there is actually another explanation: physics and, more specifically, fluid mechanics. In short, air affects scale models in a way that makes their flying behaviour more prone to sudden changes than their large scale counterparts. As a consequence, flying them requires an input capable of fast response and fast repetitions, rather than smooth and precise movements.

Handling: orientation

While the orientation of the input does not usually determine which part of the body to use, it will affect the movements of the joints in a specific way. For instance, it might allow for resting a supporting joint, making the whole experience more comfortable. Conversely, it might add an angle in the kinetic chain used for the actuation, creating discomfort for the user.

Consider two interfaces, strictly identical, each made of one unique large hand knob. While the first one is mounted vertically on a wall at a height corresponding loosely to the waist of an average person, the second one lays flat on a table.

The knob on the first interface is easy and comfortable to rotate by up to half a turn in one rotation. By contrast, the knob on the table cannot be rotated naturally and without pain by more than a quarter of a turn in one go.

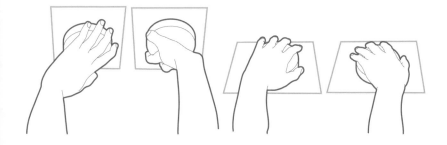

This is explained by the fact that, in the first case, the kinetic chain is (loosely) aligned with the rotation axis of the knob, whereas in the second case, whether the user is standing or sitting, the kinetic chain and the rotation axis of the knob form an angle that limits their degrees of freedom.

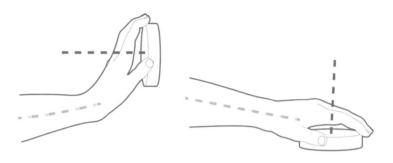

Imagine now that the two interfaces have a knob with a reduced diameter. Instead of a kinetic chain that involves all the joints from the shoulder to the fingers, the adequate kinetic chain now only involves finger joints.

In this case, both the vertical and horizontal configurations enable optimal handling, since the angle of the hand involves joints that are not directly part of the kinetic chain. Moreover, providing that there is enough space around the knob, the horizontal configuration offers added comfort by encouraging the user to rest their hand, thus offering support for the kinetic chain.

This is why it is important to make sure that scale and orientation of the input both work together to allow for successful interactions.

Handling: layout

As opposed to scale and orientation, the layout question involves all the inputs of the interface, and specifically the spacing between them. Beyond the readability and mapping of the interface, spacing allows for the user to position their palm and fingers in a way that creates new kinetic chains, thus changing the perceived characteristics of the inputs.

Consider two interfaces made of the same sliders. While the first interface is designed to be as compact as possible, the second one has plenty of space around each input.

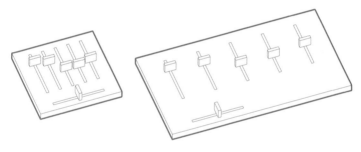

Operating the slider in the centre of the first interface without touching the other inputs involves a kinetic chain going from the shoulder to the fingers.

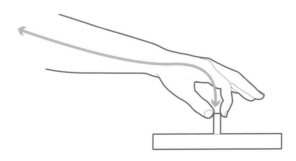

It is neither hard nor uncomfortable, but precision in small increments or decrements might prove tricky. Knowing where the slider is without looking is even harder. Now, because the second interface provides more space around the slider, it can be operated in a different manner. For instance, the palm can rest under the slider shortening the kinetic chain considerably. Better, one finger can be used to form a dynamic tripod, drastically improving precision and kinaesthetic mapping by anchoring the even shorter kinetic chain on a fixed reference point.

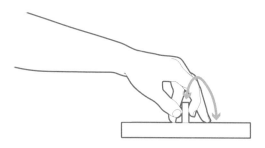

Handling: material and surface

As with the other attributes detailed previously, material and surface will undoubtedly play a role in the way the input is perceived visually. They will also influence the way the input is handled.

When confronted with a new interface, users will most likely aim for the actuation areas, usually the moving parts of the inputs they face. A change of material, colour or surface, including indents and small ridges known as 'knurls', is a good way to indicate where these actuation areas are, ensuring correct posture and encouraging the right interaction choreography.

Typically, adding a finger indent on a knob dramatically changes the interaction. Without it, users would most probably operate the knob from the outer diameter. With it, however, users are likely to place their index finger on the indent, changing both the kinetic chain and the modality of interaction to a motion that looks like the way a crank wheel is operated (unlimited rotation without interruption).

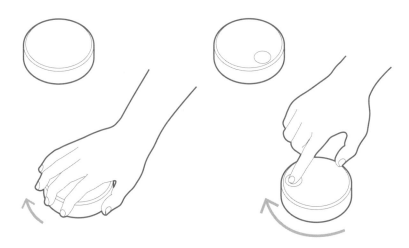

Besides their signalling function, material and surface help holding the moving part without slipping. This allows for applying less gripping force during operation, making the interaction more comfortable and potentially more precise too.

Materials can be chosen to have more or less stickiness. Surface finish, such as sanding or polishing, can be applied to make the surface grainier or, on the contrary, smoother. Finally, surface design can feature knurls and indents of all sizes and styles for various tactile sensations.

As a general rule, a stickier material and a sharper knurl design make for more grip. However, not all materials can be qualified in terms of stickiness without considering the surface finish and surface design which will also affect the overall grip in sometimes unexpected ways. Not to mention heat transmission that might make handling more or less involved whether the input feels colder (metal) or warmer (rubber, plastic and... wood). As always, prototyping various combinations remains the best way to find out.

Travel

Travel is the amplitude of movement that an input requires to be operated. In theory, inputs with short travel allow for quickly reaching any desired value while inputs with long travel allow for more precision, by putting more physical distance between any two values.

In practice, travel is determined by the scale of the input and the choice of the underlying hardware component.

Travel: hardware component

For inputs with boundaries, travel is directly determined by the architecture of the underlying hardware component. Linear and rotary potentiometers, the common components for sliders and bounded knobs respectively, are rated with a 'mechanical travel' or just 'travel', corresponding to their full range, usually in millimetres for the former and degrees for the latter.

Concerning inputs without boundaries, travel is technically unlimited. However, the operating travel, that is the average travel for the application, will be determined by the resolution of the hardware component.

The resolution of the hardware component indicates how many unique values it can return for a certain amount of travel. Rotary encoders, the common component for unlimited knobs, are usually rated with a resolution in 'pulses per rotation', the number of changes, or steps, they can detect in one full rotation.

Consider two interfaces made of unlimited knobs that look apparently the same. The first one is built using rotary encoders with a resolution of 12 pulses per rotation, while the second uses rotary encoders rated for 128 pulses per rotation. With the first interface it would take more than 10 full rotations to offer the same granularity of control to the user as the second interface accommodates for in one rotation.

So despite the fact that both interfaces feature inputs that have theoretically unlimited travel, their operating travel differs due to the difference in resolution of their respective underlying hardware components.

This is not to say that higher resolution is always better. There will be cases where the interactions work better with short travel, and cases when long travel is key. Ideally, different components should be tested to establish what feels right for a given application.

Travel: scale

Despite the overall influence of the choice of the hardware component, the exterior design of the input can also play a role in establishing the operating travel of the input. As with handling, scale is key here, albeit for different reasons.

With bounded knobs, for instance, the hardware component only determines travel in angular terms. However, knowing how much the fingers will have to move to operate the input requires converting this angular travel into linear travel.

The formula is fairly straightforward, and suffice to remember that the larger the diameter the longer travel for one given rotation.

Consider two bounded knobs using the exact same hardware component. The first one has a 5mm radius and the second a 15mm radius. The scale difference is not important enough to provoke any significant difference in the way they are handled (see *Handling: scale*), and it is fair to assume that most people would operate both knobs using two fingers. However, because the second one is 3 times larger than the first one it will effectively accommodate for 3 times more travel. As a consequence, the first knob will be faster to operate, while slightly less

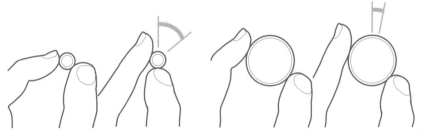

precise, and the second one will provide more precision without allowing for quite as fast changes.

With unlimited knobs, the influence of scale is slightly different. While it remains physically accurate to say that increasing the diameter increases the travel, it will not necessarily increase precision, especially if the resolution of the underlying hardware component is not adapted. Indeed, the increase of overall travel will logically increase the travel between each step. As a consequence, if the resolution was already on the low side, increasing the diameter will only make the steps more noticeable to the user without any positive effect on the precision per se.

This is why, when dealing with unlimited knobs, close attention has to be paid to resolution and handling. A small diameter knob with a low resolution is generally fine, because the way it will be handled usually allows for operating multiple rotations quickly and comfortably (see *Handling: orientation*). With the same logic, the larger the diameter, the higher the resolution should be. Only then will the influence on precision hold true.

'inputs with short travel allow for quickly reaching any desired value, while inputs with long travel allow for more precision'

Firmness

The firmness of an input describes how resistant it feels when in operation.

Instinctively, one could be tempted to think that as little resistance as possible is a good thing. However, too little resistance can equate to an input feeling 'loose', whether by poor adjustment or low manufacturing quality. And this is not only about perceived qualities. An input lacking firmness might not be physically able to accommodate the user's desire to locate and hold it before making the decision to change. It might also fail to compensate for their natural shaking. This would make it effectively less precise or, even worse, prone to be operated by mistake.

Obviously, this is not to say that firmness should always be maximised. Apart from creating discomfort, an 'over tight' input will be counterproductive for precision as it might create an elastic effect where the user has to use a force so great that each time the input is operated it starts off with a sudden jump. Firmness is about nuance, and as such it needs to be explored and tested.

In general, firmer inputs allow for more precise but slower operations, while naturally providing high kinaesthetic feedback. In contrast, looser inputs are best for less precise but faster operations with little natural kinaesthetic feedback.

As with travel, firmness is determined by the scale of the input and the choice of the underlying hardware component.

Firmness: hardware component

Amongst the first things that one should look for when selecting components to build an interface is their 'operating force', or 'operating torque' in the case of rotary components such as potentiometers and encoders.

The ratings are given in *Newtons, N* (force) or *Newton metres N.m* (torque), and characterise the quantity of friction inside a given component. The general rule is that the higher the rating, the firmer the component. However, when it comes to knowing precisely how firm it will feel, the best approach is always to prototype the interface using real components, allowing to compare, in situ, different references and manufacturers.

If all the components that have been tried feel too firm or, on the contrary, too loose, it is likely due to the scale of the input. Indeed, and as we will see in the next subsection, scale also plays a major role in the overall firmness of the input.

'firmer inputs allow for more precise but slower operations, while naturally providing high kinaesthetic feedback.'

Firmness: scale and pressure

To understand the effect played by scale on the firmness of an input, one only needs to remember two words: pressure and leverage.

Often used interchangeably, 'force' and 'pressure' do not, in reality, represent the same thing. But how they differ is actually less interesting than how they relate, especially for the question at hand.

When we press a button, how 'hard' it feels is a direct result from the pressure that needs to be exercised by our finger on the button. Interestingly, pressure equals force divided by the size of the pressing area:

$$(P = F/A),$$

meaning that the larger the button, the larger the pressing area and the easier it will feel to press.

Consider two buttons made with the same hardware component, that is with the exact same operating force rating. On the first button is mounted a 2 mm diameter cylindrical top. On the second one, the diameter is increased to 10 mm.

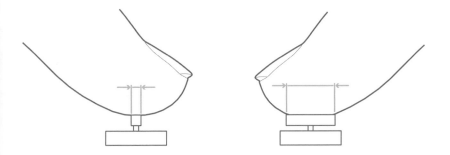

The 5 times wider design of the second button means a 25 times larger pressing surface. Now, thanks to the relation established earlier, the second button feels 25 times easier to press, with potential effects on precision and speed of operations.

This is a typical example where the exterior design of the input will have as much, if not more, influence than the choice of the underlying component on how the interaction feels.

There are, however, limits to how much playing with pressure can change the physical attributes of an input. To start with, what determines pressure is the pressing surface, not the total surface. In the previous example, had the second button been designed with a 20 mm diameter, the pressing surface would still be around 10 mm, for this is approximately the maximum contact surface of a finger.

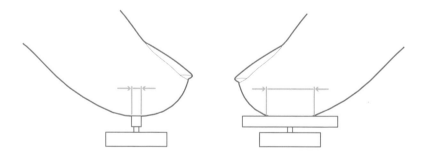

So, no change in pressure in that case. However, had this diameter been increased to 40 mm, the user might have swapped their index for their thumb (larger pressing surface), two fingers together, or even for their palm. Then the pressure would have diminished accordingly.

The second limit to pressure is that its effect is the strongest on inputs with linear or pseudo-linear actuation. For rotary inputs such as knobs, joysticks and triggers (in some implementations), leverage will be the dominating factor.

Firmness: scale and leverage

Often used metaphorically, leverage is the phenomenon through which the effect of an action is multiplied. It comes from the word 'lever', designating a bar, or stick, that we place on a pivot to move objects that would otherwise be too heavy for us to manipulate. The idea of leverage is to reduce the force necessary to perform an action by playing with distance ratios in a rotating motion. In the case of rotary inputs, leverage means that the further from the rotation centre an input is held, the easier it will be to operate.

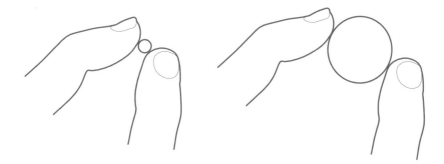

Consider two knobs made with the same hardware component, that is, with the exact same operating torque rating. The first knob has a 5 mm diameter while the second one has a 25 mm diameter. This difference does not justify any significant change in the way they are to be handled, that is mostly likely between the thumb and the index finger. However, because the second knob requires the fingers to be 5 times further away from the rotation centre, this means that it will effectively be 5 times easier to rotate than the first.

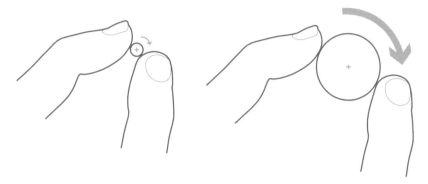

Here again, the exterior design of the input will have as much, if not more, influence than the choice of the underlying component on how the interaction feels.

Inertia

Inertia characterises the inclination of objects in motion to stay in motion, and still objects to remain still. When a bicycle is flipped upside down and the free wheel is spun to check if everything is in order, the effect of inertia is what causes it to spin long after it has last been touched.

In the case of an input, higher inertia introduces the need for an extra effort to operate it when resting, or to stop it when in operation. The effect of inertia is generally more subtle than the effects of firmness, but also more easily associated with quality. Typically, a low inertia may make the operation feel more responsive, but the overall kinaesthetic experience will be of lower quality. Conversely, a higher inertia might make the operation feel less responsive, but it will definitely enhance the overall kinaesthetic experience.

Inertia also extends the interaction possibilities. For instance, the user might accelerate the moving part of the input and let inertia maintain the motion until stopped by friction, or by the user. This comes in addition to more gentle operations and allows for dealing alternatively with low and high amplitude changes.

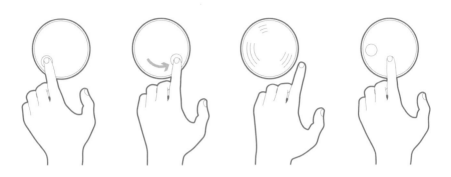

Associated with visual feedback, inertia adds predictability and sometimes expression. Common implementations include jog wheels found on most digital DJ decks and on some video editing keyboards. It is also the inspiration and conceptual model for *inertial scrolling* — software emulation of inertia — that many people use every day on their Apple devices.

'The effect of inertia is generally more subtle than the effects of firmness but also more easily associated with quality.'

Inertia: material

Inertia is largely linked to the weight of the moving part of the input. In fact, we could say that feeling the inertia of an object is mostly feeling the effect of its weight in motion. This is probably why weight is often used as an attribute of quality for higher-end interfaces (manufacturers speak of piano keyboards with 'weighted keys' or trackballs with a 'weighted ball'.).

One way to change the weight of the moving part of an input is to change its material, especially if the new material has a different material density. Material density indicates how heavy an object made of this material would be, in reference to its size. It is commonly expressed in grammes per centimetre cubed, or g/cm^3:

Wood: a bit under 1 g/cm^3
Plastic: around 1 g/cm^3
Aluminium: around 2.7 g/cm^3
Steel: around 7.8 g/cm^3.

For a given design, the denser the material of the moving part, the heavier the latter will be and the more inertia it will have.

Consider two knobs with the exact same design and exact same underlying hardware components:

- the first one is made of plastic
- the second one is made of aluminium.

Because the second knob is made of a material 2.7 times denser than plastic, it is 2.7 times heavier than the first knob and it has 2.7 times more inertia.

Inertia: scale and structure

If weight, and thus inertia, can be increased by the use of denser material, it can also be increased by increasing the scale of the moving part.

But for inputs with a rotary or pseudo rotary motion such as knobs, triggers and joysticks, *where* the weight is added is crucial: to have a significant effect on inertia, weight has to be located as far as possible from the rotation axis.

Consider three aluminium knobs with the exact same underlying hardware components and the same weight:

- the first one is full bodied with a diameter and height of 20mm

- the second one is full-bodied with a diameter of 40mm and a height of 5mm

- the third one has a hollow shape with a diameter of 40mm and a height of 20mm.

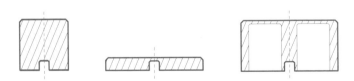

Due to the 2 times increase in diameter, the second knob has 4 times more rotational inertia than the first knob.

However, its height had to be reduced to keep the same weight, making it quite hard to operate. Interestingly, because of its hollow shape, the third knob did not require any height reduction in its design, making it great to operate. In addition, the 2 times increase in diameter allows for allocating most of the weight to the outer ring, giving it around 6 times more rotational inertia than the first knob.

Combined with material choice, changing the scale and structure of the moving part will drastically affect inertia. While still looking similar to the user, some parts can have up to 20 times more inertia than others.

Ultimately, these choices might be determined by the manufacturing process. For instance, traditional machining allows for producing full-bodied parts, whereas injection moulding usually favours parts with thin walls structures. In practice, it can be hard to control material density and internal structure independently, since each material has a preferred process. However, this is not a strict rule and the more recent manufacturing processes such as computer numerical control (CNC) machining and 3D printing allow for higher control on the structure of the parts and hence their density. Assembly is an option too, and while milling a series of knobs out of aluminium can be expensive to quickly prototype an interface, testing how inertia affects the experience can be done through comparing off-the-shelf component caps.

Feedback

When feedback is a natural attribute on an input, that is, derived from its intrinsic properties, we call it 'direct' feedback.

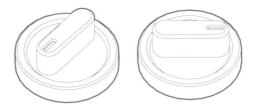

The ability to provide direct feedback depends on the chosen input concept and its physical implementation. For instance, while bounded knobs are generally good at delivering direct feedback, two bounded knobs with different travel and different firmness will not provide the same motion impression, that is direct kinaesthetic feedback, to the user.

An input with too little feedback might result in confusion and even misuse. This is the case with buttons that perform delayed actions without clear feedback such as a 'click'. This lack thereof encourages repeated pressing from the user, which can have unintended consequences on the experience.

In contrast, a good amount of feedback will ensure proper interactions, and will extend the user's natural abilities. For instance, a well-designed bounded knob on a cooking hob provides information that would not otherwise be known to the user, typically the progression of the intensity on the overall range of the hob capability. For the new user, this helps pick the right setting without having to go through trial and error and for the returning user, it allows for faster operations (it is easy to remember that 75% is the perfect setting for boiling water without risking spilling).

Sometimes, however, direct feedback is not a natural property of an input concept, or not strong enough on its own. In that case, *indirect* feedback can be added through the use of additional parts or hardware components.

In the following pages, we consider three types of feedback that can be implemented both in direct and indirect ways:

- Visual feedback
- Acoustic feedback
- Tactile & kinaesthetic feedback.

Although feedback is generally only an issue when it is lacking, there is a point where too much feedback can become a distraction or even a disturbance. This is why, as with everything else, feedback should always be prototyped and tested in real-life situations.

'a good amount of feedback will ensure proper interactions, and will extend the user's natural abilities.'

Feedback: visual

Humans have evolved to be most receptive to visual stimuli, and most users rely extensively on visual feedback in their assessment of the functioning of an interface.

Typical design features that provide direct visual feedback include uneven shapes to help notice a change in position or rotation, notches and the use of colours or markings. This is usually the case for bounded knobs where the shape or marking of the moving part indicates its rotation in reference to a scale marked on the non–moving part of the input.

With momentary or unlimited inputs, direct visual feedback is harder to implement. An uneven shape might help to see movement, but it will not provide any help when the input is idle. This is where indirect feedback comes into play. Indirect visual feedback is usually provided by the use of lights (e.g. LEDs), or a display, physically integrated inside the input (internally) or next to it (externally).

Internal integration examples include the interface of the Google Nest smart thermostat, a knob with a digital display on top, and music interfaces such as the Monome and the Novation Launchpad. The latter popularised the use of buttons with integrated LEDs for music making, allowing all sorts of new interactions and applications

Right: *Google Nest smart thermostat (2011)*

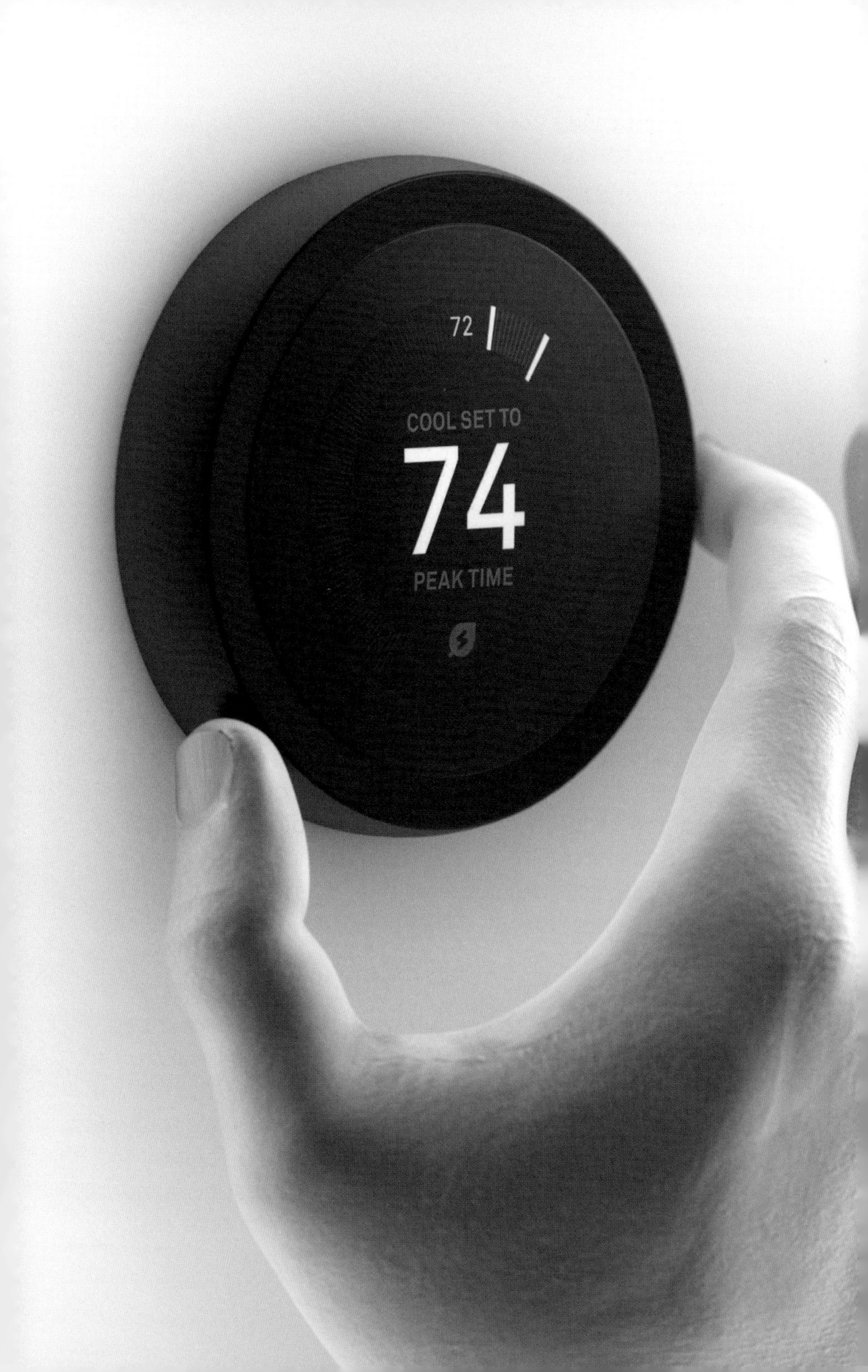
72
COOL SET TO
74
PEAK TIME

such as launching colour-mapped music clips, using their blinking on the beat to predict when they would start, or simply playing keys with scales easily identifiable through colour.

External integration is generally cheaper and more common. It usually happens on a display such as those found on home appliances and portable electronics, providing visual feedback as the inputs are being manipulated by the user.

Feedback: acoustic

As with visual feedback, the first form of acoustic feedback that can be provided is direct and mechanical.

The much sought-after 'click' is mostly the consequence of certain functional aspects of the inputs, and specifically of the architecture of the underlying hardware components. To find the right sound, the quickest approach is to compare components of different makes. Ideally, this should be done when they are mounted inside the prototype as the choice of materials and the quality of the assembly will likely induce changes in the sound propagation.

Typical inputs that have a perceptible mechanical sound include buttons, switches and knobs with detents.

For other inputs, or when direct feedback is not sufficient, indirect feedback can be added separately. Often referred to as 'audio feedback', it can be a simple 'beep' from a piezoelectric buzzer, or a more elaborate sound produced by a small integrated speaker.

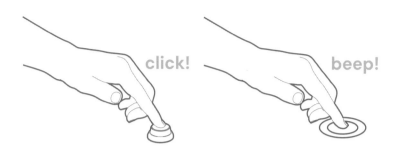

Finally, acoustic feedback can have a social function too. In some countries, a shutter sound is mandatory on digital cameras and smartphones, which usually emulate the sound of analogue cameras. This, by law, cannot be turned off to prevent pictures being taken without consent from the subject.

Feedback: tactile and kinaesthetic

While tactile feedback relates more to textures and, generally, what can be felt with the tip of a finger, kinaesthetic feedback describes our body motion impressions.

Direct tactile feedback is closely related to direct acoustic feedback: if vibrations are strong enough to generate a sound that humans can hear, they will likely be felt in our fingers too. That is why we usually associate a 'click' both with sound and with tactile sensations.

In general, the best way to find the right direct tactile and kinaesthetic feedback for a given application is to prototype the interface and try as many hardware components as possible.

However, all the other input properties covered in this chapter (handling, travel, firmness and inertia) will likely affect direct tactile and kinaesthetic feedback too. If no satisfying compromise can be found, then indirect feedback might need to be considered. In that case, it is common to use the umbrella concept of *haptic* feedback to designate both indirect tactile feedback and indirect kinaesthetic feedback, without distinction between the two.

Haptic feedback relies on the use of motors and actuators integrated inside the interface to create vibrations and forces that stimulate our tactile and kinaesthetic senses. Typical uses include simulating a click, a tap or even turbulence. On the more elaborate implementations, it can be used to help, or counter, our operation efforts in order to change, dynamically, our perception of the travel, firmness and inertia of an input. Technically referred to as force feedback, the latter is commonly found in planes and medical robots to help the operator feel how much force they are applying to the input, especially when precision is key.

Most modern gamepads feature a form of haptic feedback to add immersion to the gaming experience. In productivity it can replace functional mechanical systems. Since 2015, Apple laptops use non-clickable trackpads with haptic feedback to simulate the click, and travel. As well as the reduction of moving parts, this allows the user to adjust, through a virtual menu, the force threshold for the 'click' to be triggered, and the strength of the haptic feedback.

UX and UI considerations

The physical principles described in this chapter affect the design of graphical user interfaces in two ways:

- **Directly:** travel, feedback, and handling can all be used to change the perceived properties of a graphical user interface. Typically, the travel of a virtual slider will determine its ability for precise, if long, or responsive, if short, operations.

- **Indirectly:** as shown in the first chapter, a graphical user interface always relies on a primary (physical) interface as an entry point for user interactions. On a tablet for instance, the primary interface is usually a touch surface overlaid on a screen. For spatial computing, the primary interface is a combination of tracking inputs, sometimes with a handheld proxy device (see Chapter 5).

  Since the graphical user interface relies so heavily on the primary interface, the design of the primary interface affects the design of the graphical user interface, making it a crucial question for companies who build primary interfaces and operating systems on which graphical user interfaces will run.

Ultimately, the qualities of the interactions result from the combination of both the primary and the graphical user interfaces. To ensure that they work best together, *alignment* and *scaling* are two important factors to take into account.

UX and UI considerations: alignment

The primary interface and the graphical user interface together form an 'interface stack' and the mirroring of the inputs between the two can be described as an interaction 'alignment'. This alignment has consequences on the usability of the interface stack.

- **Maximum alignment:** a graphical user interface and a physical interface that have the exact same inputs and modalities of interaction are considered fully aligned. Typically, knobs, sliders, and buttons operated by the user on the physical interface will translate exactly into the operation of the virtual knobs, sliders, and buttons displayed on the graphical user interface. This usually makes for easily graspable interactions that allow maximum kinaesthetic mapping (every single input is physical). However, it comes at the cost of versatility, for one physical interface can theoretically only operate one graphical user interface. Moreover, in order to maintain alignment over time, software updates of the graphical user interface are constrained by the hardware of the physical interface. 'Control surfaces' for photography, film and music production are examples of physical interfaces designed for maximum alignment. Some may have a more open-ended design allowing them to connect to more than one software application and therefore multiple graphical user interfaces. This means less alignment and potentially added complexity in the overall user experience (see Chapter 6).

- **Minimum alignment:** a graphical user interface and a physical interface are unaligned when they have different inputs with different input modalities mapped to work together. Typically, a touch surface might control a bounded knob input on a graphical user interface. This offers more versatility, potentially at the cost of a limited kinaesthetic experience and sometimes frustrating interactions. Mice and trackpads are examples of physical interfaces designed with limited alignment, maximum versatility, and speed of operations. By offering comparatively more alignment than mice and trackpads, touch screens feel more intuitive to use, often giving the illusion that there is no primary interface and that the graphical user interface is the sole interface.

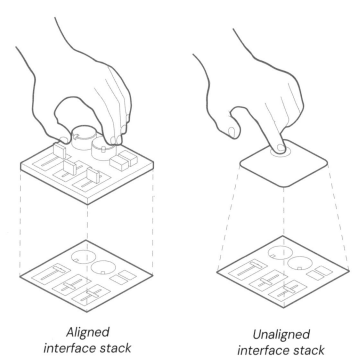

*Aligned
interface stack*

*Unaligned
interface stack*

- **Contextual alignment:** it is possible to align some inputs of the physical and the graphical user interface momentarily and in a flexible manner. This is typically what happens when the physical scroll wheel of a mouse allows for 'scrolling' through text in a window operated by a scroll bar (effectively a giant virtual scroll wheel). The contextual alignment is made possible by the 'focusing' of the physical interface on one part of the graphical user interface (here the window), through hovering the mouse pointer on top of it. Eye-tracking is increasingly used as a focusing mechanism for contextual alignment, especially for spatial computing applications. This opens the door to new design possibilities for versatile primary interfaces with specialised inputs, designed to provide great kinaesthetic sensations.

UX and UI considerations: Scale

To define the real-world dimensions of a virtual input, as experienced by the user, one needs to know the real-world dimensions at which the graphical user interface will be displayed. Apart from a few exceptions, the precise configuration of the primary interface cannot always be known with certainty, meaning that the real-world dimensions of a given virtual input may vary from one device to another. This is called 'scaling' and it can be particularly problematic with touchscreen interfaces where the user interacts by touching the virtual inputs directly. Indeed, beside affecting the overall style of the interface, this will also have an effect on the interactions since the precision, responsiveness and perceived comfort of an input can be largely dependent on its operating travel and hence, scale.

Issues of scaling commonly occur when creating virtual interfaces, since the same software on a GUI can be seen on hundreds of different types of monitors, which all have their own dimensions. Elements like text need to be a similar real-world size no matter the size of the screen, so the same paragraph might require three lines on a desktop but 12 lines on a smartphone. Finally, with devices like smartphones, where the physical interface (the touch screen) and the GUI (the lcd screen below the touch screen) are scaled to each other, it is important to consider the size of any virtual input that needs to be interacted with: a scale that worked on a larger screen may be too close on a smartphone to make a precise selection. To compensate for that, there are various strategies that can be put in place:

- **Dynamic scaling:** sometimes referred to as 'responsive design', dynamic scaling usually relies on defining rules for rescaling the interface based on known device specifications, or the display resolution, so the inputs look and behave as intended at all times. In UX and UI design, the approach has been to move away from specific values, like '500 pixels', to relational values, like placing an object in the centre of the screen.

- **Decoupling:** to avoid interaction issues due to rescaling, the visual and interactive behaviours of a given input can be 'decoupled'. For instance, upon touching, or clicking on, a virtual slider, the full screen can be used to operate it, even if the touch signal, or pointer, moves outside of the visual boundaries of said input. Another common example of decoupling is when the modality of interaction of a virtual knob is changed to *sliding* — instead of *turning* — for added comfort and precision. An added benefit of decoupling is to prevent situations where the pointer, or finger, degrades the visual feedback by constantly sitting on top of the input being operated.

- **Variable resolution:** especially with desktop computers and laptops, two interaction speeds can be defined allowing the user to choose between precision and speed through the use of left or right click, or with a modifier key.

'The primary interface and the graphical user interface together form an 'interface stack' and the mirroring of the inputs between the two can be described as an interaction "alignment".'

In practice

While the theory provides useful insights into what forms the properties of a given input, in practice the same dilemmas crop up again and again when designing interfaces: for instance, shall we favour precision over reactivity or the other way round? Finding the right balance will require making choices based on the most pressing questions for a specific use case.

In the following section there are typical questions you might ask yourself with practical advice. Beware, while some ideas can be combined, others might not be compatible. Prototyping is always a good way to find out what works best.

What if the inputs lack feedback?

General case:

- Increase the firmness: the greater the firmness, the more direct, tactile and kinaesthetic the feedback. Firmness is first determined at the component level.

- Choose shapes and markings that directly indicate the current state or value.

- Pick components with detents (or a 'click' for buttons).

- Add feedback in the form of light, sound or haptics that signal the change of state or value.

Buttons and button switches:

- Increase the firmness by decreasing the size of the contact surface.

Joysticks, triggers, knobs and other switches:

- Increase the firmness by decreasing the distance between the handling area and the pivot point of the moving part.

Right: Visual feedback for infinite knobs

What if the inputs lack expression?

General case:

- Increase the inertia: more inertia means a wider dynamic response and hence a more expressive input (e.g. piano keys). Inertia is influenced by the choice of material for the moving part: the heavier the material, the more inertia.

- Increase the inertia by increasing the size of the moving part and adapting the internal structure of the moving part: distributing the weight of the part as far as possible from the pivot point will increase inertia.

Pressure buttons:

- Increase the range of the operating force to capture all the nuances of the user 'tappings' and 'pressings'.

- Choose softer, rubbery, materials, which deform under the action of the user, hence absorbing some of the impact energy and encouraging energetic operations (e.g. drum pads). There is also a psychological element to consider: hard materials, such as glass, are perceived as fragile, inducing more cautious pressing (users are often scared of pressing too hard on their tablet touch screen, even when it is designed for pressure sensitive interactions!).

Left: Digital piano keys

What if the inputs cause discomfort or tiredness?

General case:

- Decrease the travel: the shorter the travel, the easier the operations. Travel is first determined at the component level.

- Decrease the firmness: the lower the firmness, the easier the operations. Firmness is first determined at the component level.

- Choose materials and designs that help signal where to operate and hold the input (e.g. knurling). This will translate into less effort and increased comfort.

- Make sure to leave enough space around each input in order for the user to rest their hand, fingers or wrist.

Buttons and button switches:

- Decrease the firmness by increasing the size of the moving part.

Pressure buttons:

- Decrease the minimum and maximum boundaries of the operating force, which are determined by the detection range of the hardware component.

- Choose softer, rubbery, materials, which deform under the action of the user, hence absorbing some of the impact energy and avoiding pain over repeated interactions.

Joysticks, triggers, bounded knobs and other switches:

- Decrease the travel by decreasing the distance between the handling area and the pivot point of the moving part.

- Alternatively, decrease the firmness by doing exactly the opposite!

Infinite knobs:

- If repeated rotations are frequently needed, choose designs that can be operated with two fingers: this enables a dynamic kinetic chain that favours repetitions.

- Alternatively, add a finger indent, or a finger handle, to allow for operating the moving part comfortably, as a crank wheel.

- For larger knobs, prefer vertical mounting (e.g. focus ring on a lens) allowing for repeated rotations without discomfort.

Tracking:

- Choose movements of low amplitude with short kinetic chains to avoid interactions that induce muscle fatigue.

What if the inputs are too sensitive?

General case:

- Increase the travel: the longer the travel, the less likely a value will be changed by mistake. Travel is first determined at the component level.

- Increase the firmness: the greater the firmness, the less likely a value will be changed by mistake. Firmness is first determined at the component level.

- Pick components with detents (or a 'click').

Buttons and button switches:

- Increase the firmness by decreasing the size of the contact surface.

Pressure buttons:

- Increase the minimum and maximum boundaries of the operating force, which is determined by the detection range of the hardware component.

Joysticks, triggers, bounded knobs and other switches:

- Increase the travel by increasing the distance between the handling area and the pivot point of the moving part.

- Alternatively, increase the firmness by doing exactly the opposite!

What if the inputs feel too slow or unresponsive?

General case:

- Decrease the travel: the shorter the travel, the quicker it can be to select a specific value. Travel is first determined at the component level.

- Decrease the firmness: the lower the firmness, the faster the operation of the input. Firmness is first determined at the component level.

- Choose smaller inputs: short kinetic chains are generally more suited to fast paced interactions.

Buttons and button switches:

- Decrease the firmness by increasing the contact surface of the moving part.

Pressure buttons:

- Decrease the minimum and maximum boundaries of the operating force, determined by the detection range of the hardware component.

- Avoid too soft or too rubbery a material, which would absorb, and hence delay, the 'pressing instruction' from the user.

***Overleaf:** A knob with knurls (top) and a six tracks analogue mixing console (bottom)*

Joysticks, triggers, bounded knobs and other switches:

- Decrease the travel by decreasing the distance between the handling area and the pivot point of the moving part.

- Alternatively, decrease the firmness by doing exactly the opposite!

Infinite knobs:

- Decrease the effective travel by increasing the resolution at the component level: While infinite knobs have technically unlimited travel, the effective travel (i.e. median travel for most operations) depends on the resolution of the underlying component: high resolution components require less rotations than low resolution components to offer comparable precision and reach.

Tracking:

- Choose movements of low amplitude with short kinetic chains that favour repetition.

What if you need inputs that allow for both small, precise adjustments and fast changes?

Knobs:

- Increase the inertia: higher inertia allows for dealing alternatively with low and high amplitude changes (e.g. DJ jog wheels). Inertia is influenced by the choice of material for the moving part: the heavier the material, the more inertia.

- Increase the inertia by increasing the size of the moving part and adapting the internal structure of the moving part: distributing the weight of the part as far as possible from the pivot point will increase inertia.

- Decrease the firmness at component level to avoid counteracting the effect of inertia.

- Design a knob with variable firmness and travel: This can be done by featuring two handling areas of different diameter or one continuous handling area with a variable diameter (e.g. taper). This will allow the user to intuitively adjust the travel and the firmness by the way they hold the input.

- Add a finger indent to allow for operating the input quickly, as a flat crank wheel.

Overleaf: *Native Instruments Traktor Kontrol S4 MKIII DJ decks (2018)*

Joysticks:

- Finger joysticks can offer an in-between if their lay-out allows for resting the side of the hand while operations are done with two fingers forming a kinetic chain capable of both reactivity and precision.

How to make the inputs feel higher quality?

General case:

- Increase the firmness: greater firmness gives an impression of sturdiness and quality. Firmness is first determined at the component level.

- Increase the inertia: more inertia is usually synonymous with an impression of quality. Inertia is influenced by the choice of material for the moving part: the heavier the material, the more inertia.

- Increase the inertia by increasing the size of the moving part and adapting the internal structure of the moving part: distributing the weight of the part as far as possible from the pivot point will increase inertia.

- Experiment with materials, surfaces and textures to make the inputs feel smoother or stickier, colder or warmer, softer or harder.

Teenage Engineering OP1 synthesiser, sampler and sequencer (2011)

Buttons and button switches:

- Increase the firmness by decreasing the size of the moving part.

Joysticks, triggers and bounded knobs:

- Increase the firmness by decreasing the distance between the handling area and the pivot point of the moving part.

Infinite knobs:

- Adapt the travel of the moving part to the resolution of the hardware component to prevent the user from noticing steps in the returned values: The lower the resolution the smaller the diameter should be.

What if the inputs lack precision?

General case:

- Increase the travel: the longer the travel, the easier it is to select a specific value. Travel is first determined at the component level.

- Increase the firmness: an input lacking firmness might be hard to locate and hold. Firmness is first determined at the component level.

- Choose larger inputs: whole hand operations imply strong kinetic chains that favour stable movements and precision.

- If the interface only allows smaller inputs, make sure to leave enough space around each in order for the user to rest their hand, fingers or wrist, allowing shorter kinetic chains and increased precision.

- Increase the grip on the moving part with a rougher material or design (e.g. knurling) to ensure optimal operation, and increased precision.

Joysticks, triggers and bounded knobs:

- Increase the travel by increasing the distance between the handling area and the pivot point of the moving part.

- Alternatively, increase the firmness by doing exactly the opposite!

Infinite knobs:

- Increase the resolution: resolution is determined at the component level.

Rolling inputs (e.g. mouse or trackball) and touch surfaces:

- Choose smoother materials and surface finish for added precision (undesired friction can cause jumps).

Tracking:

- Choose movements of high amplitude with long kinetic chains that allow for control and precision.

What if this is not enough?

Occasionally, you will find that your interface still lacks a little something to accommodate for the intended interactions. This can be especially frustrating when all the design possibilities — within the constraints of the project — have been explored. In that case, it is likely the right time to start looking at the 'behaviour' of the various inputs that form your interface.

Right: *Tapered knob*

void Update ()
{
xPanFiltered =
ivedValue * (1f - lowPassRatio);
yPanFiltered =
ivedValue * (1f - lowPassRatio);
if (Mathf.Abs (xP
panThreshold || Mathf.Abs (yPanF
- lastYPanReadi
{
isPanning =
alse)
}
if
{
}
}

4/ Behaviour Concepts

While the various input concepts we have seen in the previous chapters follow general rules that distinguish them from one another, there are different ways their returned state, or signal, can be interpreted to form an output. This gives *fluidity* to their behaviour, ultimately making them more versatile than they might initially appear to be. This interpretation happens through the execution of a program that will convert the state or signal returned by the input into an output state or signal.

In theory, the execution of this program can happen at firmware or software level, the former being more specialised, and potentially faster, as it is embedded in the hardware components, and the latter being more versatile, and potentially more suited for complexity, as it runs on a computer.

In practice, choosing one over the other will depend on the precise interaction needs and the technical specification of the interface. When it comes to prototyping, both approaches are reasonably accessible: behaviours can be prototyped as firmware using a development board such as an Arduino, or as software using any personal computer or a single-board computer such as a Raspberry Pi.

Finally, while the diagrams presented in this chapter are fully implementable, they are simplified for the purpose of illustrating the general logic of these behaviours.

Switch behaviour

As we have seen before, the switch is an input concept on its own that can take different forms, all sharing the characteristic of displaying their state physically in a more or less obvious way. Sometimes, however, a simple button can be programmed to *act* as a switch. Whether motivated by economic reasons, or just because it is a more flexible solution, the idea is to store in memory a digital state that can be swapped for the next state every time the button is pressed.

Consider the example of a bicycle light that only has one button:

- By default, the state is 'OFF' (no light)

- If the user presses the button once, it activates the next state: 'low light' (the light switches on at 50% intensity)

- If the user presses again it activates the next state: 'strong light' (the intensity of the light increases to 100%)

- If the user presses the button again, it goes back to the initial state: 'OFF' (light switches off)

- If the user presses the button again, the cycle starts again.

In this example, we have a simple button that is effectively used as a 3 state switch. On one hand, it is more versatile than using an actual switch, because states can be added or removed without having to modify the hardware. On the other hand, it does not provide feedback or mapping of the different states to the user who can only 'try and see' (or perhaps, read the instruction manual).

Here is a typical implementation:

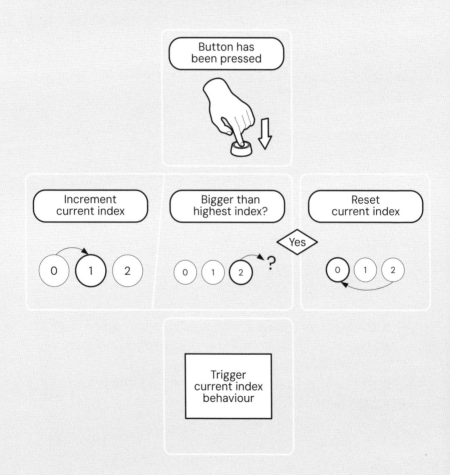

Please note that it requires defining how many states are needed and assigning them an index starting from 0.

Index	State
0:	'OFF'
1:	'low light'
2:	'strong light'

This behaviour can be assigned to other input concepts. For instance, it could work with a trigger or a (non-maintained) joystick. For the latter, we could have an implementation where one side of the joystick activates the *next* state, while the other side activates the *previous* state (useful when there are many states).

'a simple button … is more versatile than … an actual switch, because states can be added or removed without having to modify the hardware. '

Double-press

Ubiquitous with human-computer interactions, the double-press (or double-*click*), is probably the most commonly used 'smart' behaviour. The basic idea is to allow for directly performing two distinct actions with one input. On most computers these two actions are 'select' (single-click) and 'open' (double-click). However nothing prevents implementing a double-press behaviour for other purposes.

Keeping the one button bicycle light example, we can imagine the following:

- Single-press allows for switching between the 'ON' and 'OFF' states (see *Switch behaviour*)

- Double-press allows for switching between the different light intensity states (see *Switch behaviour*).

On the opposite page, we see a typical implementation.

Beware: the devil is in the details. Too small a delay might not give enough time for slower users to perform a double-click/double-press. Too long a delay might create 'false positives' (user tries to perform 2x single-press actions that are interpreted as a double-press). Worse still, it can make the interactions feel not responsive enough (no decision can be made until the delay has elapsed).

Please note that double-press can be used with other input concepts too. With a trigger, it could be used as a modifier: for instance, if the user double-squeezes it, we could have the output multiplied by x (instead of output values going from 0 to 1 with a single squeeze, they could go from 0 to x in that case).

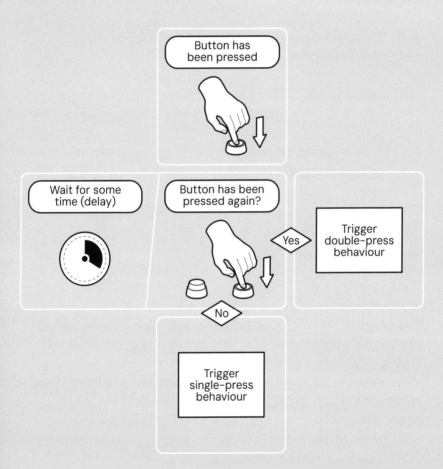

Long-press

Similar to the double-press, long-press is a way to offer a distinct interaction to those activated by a normal (i.e. short) press.

With the one button bicycle light example, we can imagine the following:

- Long-press allows for switching between the 'ON' and 'OFF' states (see *Switch behaviour*)

- Single-press allows for switching between the different light intensities

- Double-press allows for switching between the different blinking frequencies.

On the opposite page, we see a typical implementation.

Again, beware of false positives. Also, as we can see on this diagram, how *frequently* this function can be run is key to reduce the risk of a fast press going undetected. This is why running it directly on the firmware might be more reliable. Indeed, the reading frequency of firmware is likely to be much higher than the reading frequency of software which will also need to account for the frequency of the communication protocol used between the firmware and the software.

To mitigate that issue, some firmware can flag specific events when they occur. So instead of a 'dumb' communication where the software can only ask the firmware if the user *is pressing* at the moment, events allow for the software to ask the firmware if the user *has pressed* the button since they last communicated.

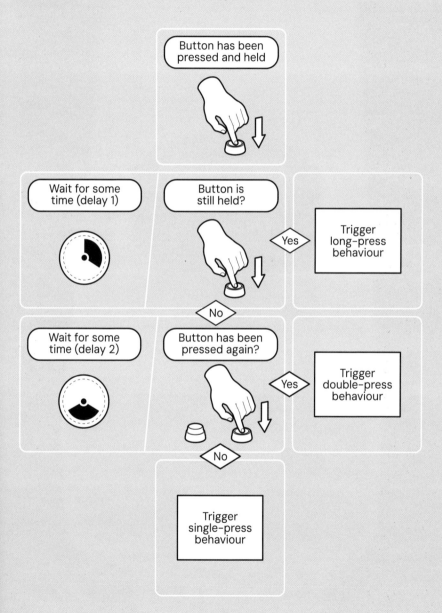

Dynamic response

With unbounded input concepts, the question of the resolution is often central to delivering a satisfying user experience. However, not all hardware offers the same resolution and, logically, higher resolution often comes at a higher price point. But hardware is not the only limiting factor, and we humans are also limited in our capacity to move our fingers in space with precision — especially when it comes to small movements. Of course, the resolution can always be digitally multiplied to offer more control. This is typically what happens when a user sets the 'tracking speed' of their mouse or trackpad to 'slow'. However, while it allows for more precise operation, it also makes everything feel … slow.

The concept of 'dynamic response' comes in to overcome this limitation. The idea is simple: understand what the user is trying to achieve (e.g. *quick* change or *precise* modification) and adapt the digital multiplication of the resolution accordingly so as it always feels right: *fast* when precision is not needed, or *precise* when speed does not matter.

As often with behaviour concepts, time is the key variable that will allow for inferring the user's intention. By continuously measuring the speed at which an input is being operated, we multiply the output accordingly to create a dynamic behaviour.

Consider the example of a bicycle light that has a continuous knob instead of a button:

- If the user turns the knob *quickly*, every degree of rotation corresponds to 1 percentage point of light increase (or decrease if anticlockwise). In other words, the user can turn the light from 0% to 100% intensity with a bit more than a quarter of a turn (100 degrees).

- Now, if the user turns the knob *slowly*, every degree of rotation corresponds to 0.1 percentage point of light increase (or decrease), making the operation 10 times more precise than when the knob is turned quickly.

On the opposite page, we see two implementations (above without threshold, below with).

Limiting the minimum/maximum output values, or using a threshold can help make it more predictable to the user. Conversely, squaring the speed in the output calculation can make it feel even more responsive. It can also be adapted to buttons by measuring the *frequency* at which they are pressed and changing their output accordingly (common in video games).

Ultimately, nothing beats testing it in a situation and with the final hardware specification.

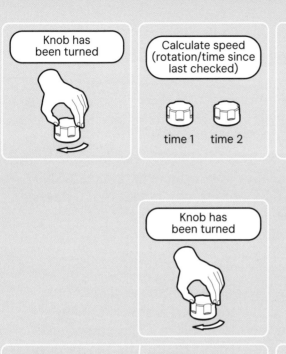

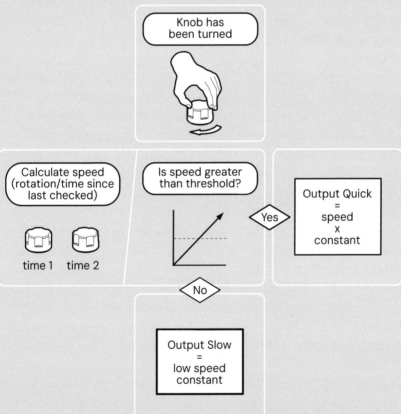

Inertia

While most of the behaviour concepts described here are very much rooted in the modern history of interfaces, physical inputs that allow for playing with inertia are fairly rare in the real world (see Chapter 3). Yet, it is one of the most popular behaviour concepts. This is maybe due to the fact that it connects to something much deeper in the human brain: our ability to naturally anticipate the movement of objects without having to formally understand the underlying laws of physics.

Its first large-scale use came with the original Apple iPhone in 2007, which introduced 'inertial scrolling' (sometimes called 'kinetic scrolling'). The core idea is that the returned value is still affected by the input after the user has stopped interacting with it, and slowly decreases to reach zero. In the case of the iPhone, the user initiates the scrolling with a swipe and can see the scrolling continue on its own. The user can then stop the scrolling with a single touch or let it slow down and stop on its own. This is supposed to mimic the real-world behaviour of objects that upon being pushed will move due to their *inertia* until they eventually come to a halt under the combined effects of friction and gravity (e.g. sliding a hockey puck on an ice surface).

The immediate success of this concept can be explained by its playfulness, extreme intuitiveness and actual usefulness (small thumb movements allow for amplified movements on the screen). Not unlike the dynamic response concept, it offers a way for the user to alternate between *fast*, *large* changes and *slow*, *precise* adjustments.

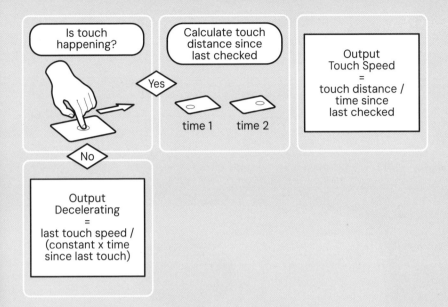

Above, we see a typical implementation.

Beware, inertia, *as a behaviour concept*, will only be able to build on the user's natural ability to anticipate movement where there is a notion of ... movement! As such, while you could imagine implementing inertia with other input concepts such as infinite knobs, triggers, joysticks or even buttons, it should always be associated with visual feedback and a clear conceptual model. In the previous bicycle light example, inertia would only make operating the light confusing unless, maybe, associated with a decent resolution monitor and a progression bar. Even then, such an interaction model would be hard to justify as there would be no clear benefit to it. Ultimately, if the input you have designed already features noticeable physical inertia (see Chapter 3), adding *behavioural* inertia (i.e. at firmware or software level) is likely to induce odd conflicts of interactions.

Filtering

Inputs that provide a continuous signal are prone to undesirable value jumps that happen even when the input is not in operation. These fluctuations are referred to as 'noise' and are usually due to the way electricity flows within the underlying hardware components. In addition to noise, and especially as the resolution of these components increases, another type of undesirable value instability can appear, this time due to the user's natural tendency to shake. The latter is particularly noticeable with tracking inputs encouraging free-handed movement, that is, with little support for the kinetic chain involved. If the application involves the manipulation of a virtual object in 3D, the combined effect of signal noise and shaking might cause said object to suddenly jump from one position to another in a distracting manner.

A common way to avoid these undesired fluctuations is to filter the signal by removing the smaller sudden changes, *assumed to be unintentional*. A basic and yet efficient way to do that is to weight each incoming value returned by the input against an average of the previous ones.

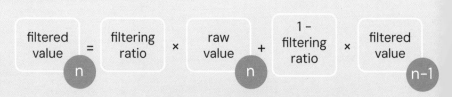

$$\text{filtered value}_n = \text{filtering ratio} \times \text{raw value}_n + (1 - \text{filtering ratio}) \times \text{filtered value}_{n-1}$$

The less weight (smaller ratio) given to the incoming signal (raw values), the smoother the filtered signal.

While simple to implement, this filtering method will introduce delay proportionally to the amount of filtering. This might make the interaction feel less reactive and may reduce the granularity of control for the user. If no compromise can be found to significantly reduce the effects of noise or shaking without negatively affecting the experience, more advanced filtering methods and higher quality components may need to be considered (the latter will only have an effect on noise).

'this filtering method will introduce delay proportionally to the amount of filtering. This might make the interaction feel less reactive and may reduce the granularity of control for the user.'

5/ Combined Concepts

In the previous chapters we have considered each input concept and its implementation as an individual entity. In practice, unless extremely specialised or minimalistic, an interface is rarely limited to one single input.

In this chapter we bring the focus to input combinations, some common and some more surprising, to show how bringing individual input concepts together can lead to the emergence of original properties and new interaction modalities.

For the most part, these combinations are described as concepts and, as such, can entail different physical realities. While some might be readily available as off-the-shelf components requiring little adaptation, others will require custom design and engineering. In the latter case, the way individual components are brought together plays a key role in the overall functionality of the combined concept.

D-pad

Combines: button inputs together (usually four)

While a button alone can only trigger a predefined action, or be used as a switch (see Chapter 4), two buttons can control a value, one being used to increment and the other to decrement. With the same principle, four buttons can control two values, or a two-dimensional one. In a cross arrangement, this is called a d-pad (for 'directional' pad) that can either be designed with the four buttons under one body or be kept physically separated. While considered somewhat similar to a joystick, a d-pad accommodates for discrete increments, or decrements, instead of a true continuous signal. That translates into potentially less granularity, but faster operations, and, in some cases, more precision (each button is either returning 1 or 0). Moreover, if the d-pad is made of four separated buttons, they can all be operated at the same time, which is not possible with a joystick.

For this reason, the d-pad is common on gamepads, instead of, or in addition to, a joystick. It is also perfectly suited for basic menu navigation such as what can be found on car audio systems, TV remotes and monitors.

Left: Nintendo Gameboy (1989)

Click-knob

Combines: infinite knob + button inputs

In its simplest form, the click-knob is an infinite knob mounted on a button. If this button is programmed to act as a switch (see Chapter 4), one single click-knob can alternatively control two or more parameters. Visual feedback is usually a welcome addition, if only to know which parameter is currently targeted by the click-knob.

Associated with a monitor and a graphical user interface, it is an efficient combined input for one-dimensional navigation, as demonstrated by the click-knob (called 'Digital Crown') on the Apple Watch and Apple Vision Pro devices.

Another version of the click-knob sees four additional buttons arranged in a cross inside, outside or beneath the knob, itself usually designed to be operated frontally. Commonly referred to as a 'click-wheel', it has the properties of both the simpler click-knob and of the d-pad. This combined concept was made popular by the first Apple iPod released in 2001, and has had many evolutions, including the replacement of the mechanical knob by a circular touch surface input. Nowadays it is still commonly found on digital cameras where it allows for menu navigation.

Left: *Apple Watch Series 7 (2021)*

Keyboard and keypad

Combines: button inputs together (10 - 100+)

Numerical keypads enable the composition of numbers whether for calculation, making a phone call or using a combination lock. With up to 110 buttons, or keys, not only does a keyboard allow for typing, it also enables complex interactions with computers using language (command lines and programming) and kinaesthetic memory (shortcuts).

Interestingly, lesser known variations featuring only five buttons have long existed alongside the more densely populated keyboard that are usually associated with computers. Despite being much smaller and portable, these allow for a wide range of computer interactions, including typing, following a logic similar to how piano keys can be combined to form chords. Hence their name: 'chorded keyboards'. Such designs still exist today, albeit in a smaller market segment.

Left: *Keychron K8 wireless mechanical keyboard (2020)*

Mouse

Combines: rolling + button inputs (+ miscellaneous)

Often considered as an input on its own, the mouse is the quintessential combined input. The emergence of new properties from the seemingly simple association of a travel input with a button input enabled computing to reach a wider audience by transitioning from command-line interactions to the more visual 'windows, icons, menus, pointer' paradigm still in use four decades after being popularised by the introduction of the Apple Macintosh in 1984.

While the first commercial units (1973's Xerox Alto mouse and 1981's Xerox Star mouse) already included multiple buttons, various designs have existed and still coexist today with as little as one button and often an additional input on top. The latter is commonly an infinite knob, usually called a 'scroll wheel', but Apple's designs used to feature a mini trackball instead, until it was replaced by a touch surface on the latest Apple mice.

Nowadays, the trackpad, which replaces the mouse for most laptop users, is a variation of the same idea (touch surface + button inputs) thus providing similar functionalities even if their properties and interaction modalities differ slightly.

Left: A vertical mouse (top), a Redragon gaming mouse (middle right), a Logitech mouse (middle left) and an Apple mouse (bottom)

3D mouse

Combines: joystick + knob + pressure button inputs

While sharing a similar form factor with the traditional mouse and being intended for a comparable use, the 3D mouse builds on a singularly different stack of inputs and, logically, works in a completely different way. While the former is designed for 2D operations with effectively 2 to 3 degrees of freedom, the latter offers 6 degrees of freedom, the possibility to translate and rotate an object along 3 axes.

3D mice have been through many iterations and prove popular within specific segments of the 3D modelling market. As for day-to-day operations such as navigating a web browser, they can be much harder to use than traditional mice, which benefit from the stability property of the travel input. In fact, a 3D mouse is often used in conjunction with a traditional mouse, one hand being dedicated to 3D manipulation and the other focusing on more traditional pointing, clicking and menu navigation.

Left: 3Dconnexion SpaceMouse Wireless (2013)

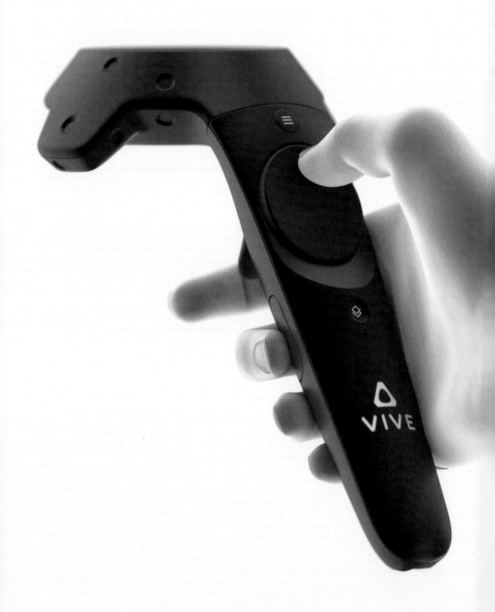

Motion controller

Combines: tracking + button inputs (+ miscellaneous)

Although the idea of using body motion as a new type of input has been around for decades, the 2006 Nintendo Wii Remote is usually regarded as the first commercially successful handheld interface combining tracking and button inputs.

Nowadays, most video game controllers have effectively become motion controllers and it seems to be the combined input of choice for spatial computing. In the latter case, it should be noted that hand tracking is often perceived as a more 'natural' interaction mechanism. Interestingly, the debate between the supporters of the motion controller and those of hand tracking is in many ways reminiscent of the dispute between the partisans of stylus interactions and those of finger interactions when touch screens started becoming popular (which echoes the arguments of those preferring the mouse, or the trackpad). Ultimately, there are applications where interactions that do not require holding a motion controller feel more practical, or 'natural', and others where holding one extends the user's abilities (e.g. by stabilising hand movements).

Left: HTC Vive controller (2016), used for virtual reality applications

Headsets

Combines: tracking + button inputs (+ miscellaneous)

Looking at a virtual reality headset, one can be tempted to think of a computer monitor strapped on someone's head. After all, the quality of the display and its pixel resolution capture a lot of the attention and one tends to forget that what makes the magic happen is the fact that the headset is, firstly, a perfectly adjusted, and calibrated, interface.

Indeed, for the user to think, not that they are looking at a display, but rather travelling in another world, a virtual camera has to mimic the exact movements of the user's head. And this is even more crucial with spatial computing and mixed reality, where the smallest misalignment can break the illusion that virtual objects are part of the user's space. These movements are tracked in real time, using a combination of tracking inputs usually integrated in the headset where they are synchronised with the tracking of the user's hands, or of a motion controller, to enable spatially sound interactions with virtual objects.

Left: Apple Vision Pro headset (2024)

6/ Interface Stories

In the following stories we look at the evolution of selected interfaces in order to see how seemingly small changes, or bigger ones, such as the introduction of digital technologies, can have a dramatic impact on the user's perception of machines and their ability to interact with them. Only one of the four stories specifically relates to computer interfaces. However, computers play a role in three of them, illustrating the profound impact that these machines have had, directly or indirectly, on the way people think about interactions and the design of interfaces.

Human computer interfaces

Surprisingly, computers were not exactly *interactive* until the mid 1950s, with the introduction of the first personal computers — literally computers that could be used by one *person* directly and without sharing. Before that, a computer operator would be in charge of inputting and running instruction batches for other people who would have to wait for hours, sometimes days, to see the results of their computing. A device called the teleprinter, used to send and receive typed messages, was at the centre of this process, and its interface, the keyboard, was logically kept as the first interface for interacting directly with personal computers.

RFT 51a – PL 2
teleprinter (1930-1940)

Until the early 1980s, language remained the main input concept and typing (commands) the main interaction modality for operating a computer. Many books, articles and movies have recounted the story of Steve Jobs insisting on the mouse and the graphical user interface being part of the Apple Lisa after having been inspired by a demonstration at Xerox's Palo Alto Research Centre.

Left: *Apple Macintosh*
personal computer (1984)

Yet, it is hard to grasp how instrumental this decision has been to the rise of the computer as a truly personal device. This unique interface combination would change the meaning of the personal computer idea, with machines increasingly designed to appeal to the general user rather than only target the expert technician.

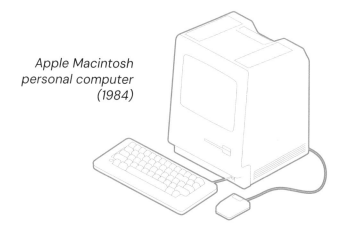

Apple Macintosh personal computer (1984)

While command lines were more suited to complex or repetitive tasks with functionalities that could be unlimited, the graphical user interface associated with a pointing mechanism allowed anyone to quickly grasp what they could do through metaphorical representations and functionalities such as the 'desktop', the 'windows' and the 'drag and drop'. It opened the doors to more visual and intuitive applications, allowing software developers such as Adobe to develop an offering that would bring new audiences, famously the creative industry professionals, to the personal computer.

Over the years, the growing popularity of the touch surface input helped grow the computer interface landscape, first with the trackpad, and later the touch screen. Besides offering a solid alternative to the mouse for portable devices, they enabled a new interaction modality with touch gestures including the 'swipe', 'pan' and 'pinch' gestures.

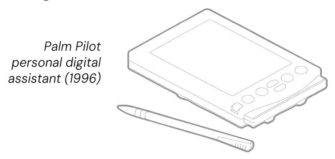

Palm Pilot personal digital assistant (1996)

While command-line interactions never disappeared for expert applications, it took several attempts for the idea of using language as a system-wide input concept to make a comeback.

In 2006, Microsoft introduced Windows Speech Recognition, allowing for controlling certain aspects of the Windows operating system via voice commands, and in 2011 Apple launched Siri, a voice assistant that would soon be part of all Apple devices. Gradually, the user could move away from their monitor and speak casually to their computer, which was able to perform 'speech recognition' and 'natural language processing' to respond adequately. While the idea of conversational interactions had been developed in the mid 1960s with the ELIZA program at the Massachusetts Institute of Technology, rapid progress in 'machine learning' at the turn of the 2010s made it a much more versatile solution for general interactions. Chatbots started appearing for all types of applications and, in 2014, Amazon released Echo, usually believed to be the first 'smart speaker', a form of simplified computer, designed to function solely around language as an input.

While retaining some of the core characteristics of the command line interaction mechanism, including the ability to offer a large number of options without having to organise them in menus, these more recent implementations of language do not require learning a specific syntax or computer logic. In that sense, it gives another dimension to the very idea of human–machine interactions which increasingly resemble interactions between humans.

Amazon Echo smart speaker (2014)

However, spoken commands and, to some extent, typed ones, also raise privacy concerns since artificial intelligence makes them increasingly at risk of being recorded and reverse engineered. Moreover, language proceeds exclusively from logical thinking when visual and physical interfaces can accommodate abstract intellectual processes.

As a result, it can be limiting where discoverability and kinaesthetic memorisation are concerned, and less suited for some activities where creative exploration is necessary.

In the end, modern computers can use a number of input concepts and interfaces, allowing for a variety of interaction modalities suited for users based on their needs. Paradoxically, it makes adoption of newer technologies such as glasses or headsets for spatial computing slower, since they tend to rely on a more limited set of inputs.

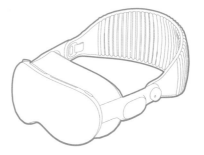

Apple Vision Pro headset (2024)

Some aspects of computer interactions, such as the often overlooked keyboard shortcuts, will need to be reimagined in these new contexts.

'Some aspects of computer interactions, such as the often overlooked keyboard shortcuts, will need to be reimagined in these new contexts.'

Camera lenses

For decades, camera lenses required photographers to set the focus manually, by turning a ring — the *focus* ring — which would mechanically adjust the distance between the different glass elements of the lens.

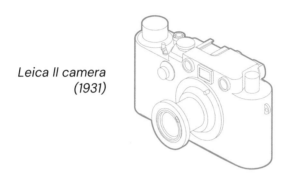

Leica II camera
(1931)

In the late 1970s, Leica introduced the 'autofocus', a mechanism to measure the camera–to–subject distance and set the focus accordingly. Over the years, the technology progressed and entry level cameras became fully automated. However, users of higher–end equipment generally remained attached to keeping the possibility of focusing their lenses manually, whether for precision, creative control or just the kinaesthetic experience.

This is why, for a long time, most lenses apart from compact camera lenses, kept a 'manual–first' design. The autofocus had come as an *additional* functionality, logically bringing extra production cost, weight and potential sources of failure. It was only time before a manufacturer would try to flip the equation.

Left: *Leica M3 (1954)*

Named after the 'fly-by-wire' technology that saw mechanical flight control systems in planes evolve into electrical ones, 'focus-by-wire' followed a similar idea: replace the mechanical interface providing direct manual control of the focus with an electronic command system only allowing for *indirect* manual control, via a little motor. This enabled building an optimal autofocus with a simplified internal architecture and reduced size, thus avoiding potential conflicts of command between the user and the automation mechanism.

Airbus A320 plane equipped with fly-by-wire commands (1984)

Initially only present on avant-garde lenses such as that of the 1999 Sony DSC-F505 bridge camera, focus-by-wire went mostly unnoticed throughout the 2000s. The real turning point occurred in the early 2010s following the boom in mirrorless cameras due to a growing appetite from photographers for devices able to shoot both still images and video. Mirrorless cameras such as the Panasonic Lumix DMC-G series were significantly smaller than their Digital Single Lens Reflex (DSLR) counterparts and specifically suited for video thanks to a fully exposed sensor. Great for video autofocus and small by nature, focus-by-wire lenses appeared as the logical companion of mirrorless cameras and, together, they became a new standard in photography equipment.

Sony DSC-F505 camera (1999)

In 2021, Sony announced the end of their DSLR line to focus solely on their flagship mirrorless series born only 8 years before with the a7. Other manufacturers have made similar moves and today, focus-by-wire is arguably the main lens technology for dedicated camera equipment.

Sony a7 mkIII camera (2018)

If one takes a close look at a modern focus-by-wire lens, it is apparent that much effort has been put into preserving the design language of traditional mechanical lenses. For manual focusing, a ring designed to *look* like a mechanical focus ring is used to send rotation instructions to a little motor taking care of the actual focusing. On most implementations, the response of the ring is dynamic, based on user settings or the speed at

While they look similar to traditional lenses, focus-by-wire lenses (below right) do not have any marking on the rings

which the 'focus ring' is rotated (see *Dynamic response* in Chapter 4). Typically, a quick rotation of 20 degrees might be interpreted as an instruction to move the focus by 20 metres, while a *slow* rotation of the exact same 20 degrees might be interpreted as an instruction to move the focus by 20 millimetres only.

In theory, this can provide faster and finer control than with traditional lenses. In practice, it comes at a certain cost, especially from the perspective of the user experience.

To start with, because a dynamic response requires boundless rings, it makes it impossible to keep the traditional focus distance markings on the lens barrel. Yet, these markings are a great way to provide visual feedback to the user. At times, for instance in dark environments, focusing a lens manually using markings can be the quickest way to achieve a satisfying focus.

In addition, an input with a dynamic response has no concept of mapping, meaning that there is no linear correlation between the rotation of the focus ring and the position of the focus plane. This is typically a limitation for filmmaking where manual focusing, usually referred to as 'focus pulling', is an integral part of the crafting of the image. To that end, mapping is essential, as muscle memory allows the person focusing the lens to instinctively know how the focus is moving and to make beautiful focus transitions. The unpredictability of dynamic response can make focus-by-wire lenses much harder to use than traditional lenses in such use cases, which is slightly ironic considering that mirrorless cameras and focus-by-wire lenses were largely developed with video in mind.

Each new generation of focus-by-wire lenses comes with new hardware developments, finer calibration and improved physical design. Photographers are getting used to the feel of dynamic focusing too even if it still sparks fierce debates amongst them. In the end, many just enjoy the inherent robustness of the autofocus that focus-by-wire architecture has been designed to provide. Moreover, they always have the option to use real — *purely manual* — lenses, which remain popular with frequent releases from historical manufacturers such as Voigtländer.

The lens is a great illustration of how the use of a seemingly simple object is in fact largely influenced by interface design decisions. By only looking at one aspect, the focus ring, this story allows for establishing how much a technological change can affect the interactions, even if much effort is spent to retain the historical characteristics of said interface. In 'fooling' the users by emulating mechanical lenses as closely as possible, focus-by-wire lenses were initially deemed the *least* usable (because they weren't close enough to the original). Conversely, with the introduction of dynamic response, they lost the possibility for markings and mapping, but also enabled real fine control and fast operation when needed.

This illustrates the fact that designers should not just try to imitate great interactions but, instead, they should break down what the fine characteristics of an interaction are, in order to build the best interface possible within the imposed technological constraints. Here, one would almost wish to have witnessed an alternative design history where manufacturers went further and proposed a clearly different interface, allowing for new types of interaction modalities that *embraced* the change of the technological paradigm. For instance, there could have been designs with two or three rings, each offering a different focus speed; or a ring with a slider and knob mechanism where fast focus adjustment would have been done in translation, and fine focusing in rotation.

'designers should not just try to imitate great interactions but, instead, they should break down what are the fine characteristics of an interaction in order to build the best interface possible within the imposed technological constraints.'

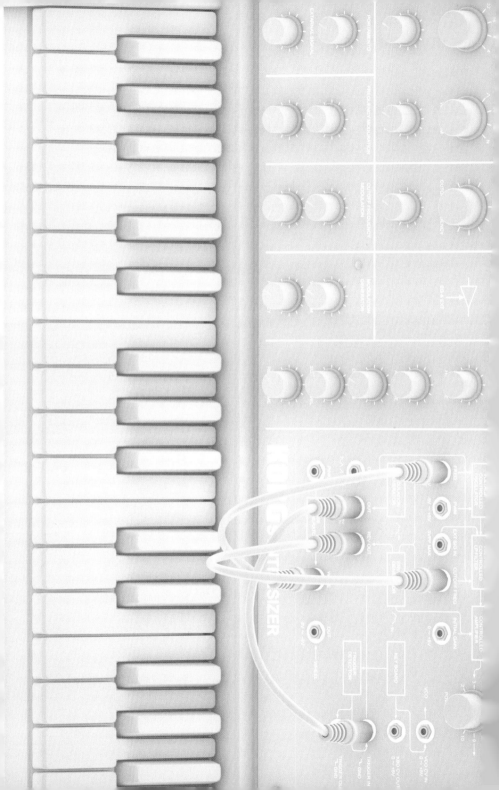

Music making interfaces

Branching out from a 60,000 year old lineage of apparatuses making use of mechanical phenomena to produce melodies, synthesisers appeared in the first half of the twentieth century owing to the advent of electricity and, later, electronics.

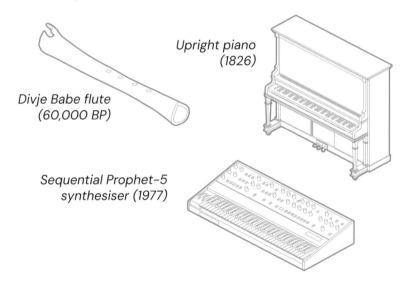

*Upright piano
(1826)*

*Divje Babe flute
(60,000 BP)*

*Sequential Prophet–5
synthesiser (1977)*

Due to the way they combined circuits to *synthesise* sound, these machines introduced a new creative avenue to the musician, that is, the possibility to craft their own sounds through interfaces with complex–looking designs as a direct result of the underlying electronic circuits they controlled. Interestingly, this type of interface, informed by necessity, would become ubiquitous with the very idea of modern music making, especially electronic music.

***Left:** Korg MS–20
synthesiser (1977)*

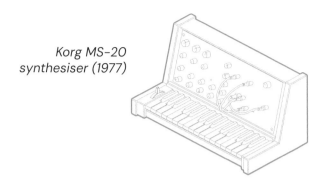

*Korg MS-20
synthesiser (1977)*

Audio recording evolved too and the late 1980s saw
the emergence of the Digital Audio Workstation (DAW),
a multitrack recording and mixing console emulated
through a software application. Finally, it took another
decade for software synthesis and sampling to be
considered a credible alternative to physical instruments.
By the late 1990s, a DAW could be used to compose,
arrange and mix a multi-track piece on a personal
computer without the need for any musical instruments
or other forms of equipment.

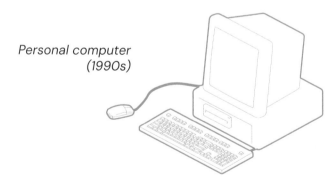

*Personal computer
(1990s)*

In a nutshell, one century of technology evolution had
not only resulted in the introduction of new instruments
and advanced recording equipment, but also in their
dematerialisation through software emulation, with added
benefits such as non-destructive recording and infinite

rearrangement. All of this was accessible to anyone for the cost of a personal computer and a software licence. The story could have ended there, and physical instruments could have turned into decorative artefacts from a distant past. Instead, it backtracked and changed course. And it did so for an *interface* question.

While the idea of having a whole music studio in a laptop was certainly interesting on paper, from an interaction perspective, however, it meant reducing the whole choreography of music composition and performance to 'clicking' and 'scrolling'. Besides being somewhat uninspiring, this also created impractical situations where simple interactions such as turning a few knobs would require unjustified effort for a less precise result.

To solve these issues, music equipment manufacturers such as Akai and Korg started to produce affordable 'control surfaces', effectively physical interfaces designed to allow musicians to take advantage of the DAW-centric workflow through dedicated interactions. These interfaces met with certain success, but paradoxically suffered from being designed to be compatible with the widest range of DAW applications. While honourable in its ambition, this open-ended design meant musicians would often have to spend precious time setting up their physical interface to synchronise properly with the virtual one on the screen. Moreover, the amount of interactions covered by these interfaces would be limited, and the recurring need to reach for the mouse or keyboard would often result in losing one's focus and ideas. This set the stage for a new generation of physical interfaces designed, from the ground up, to work with one specific software application and hence, one graphical user interface (see Chapter 3).

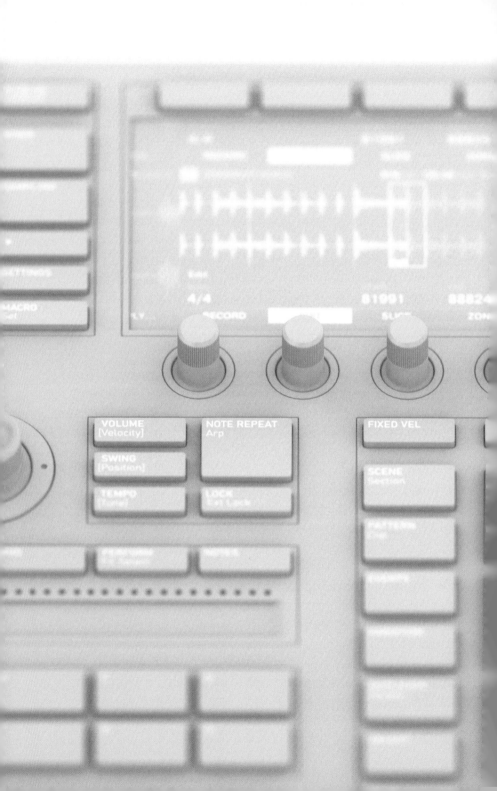

The 2009 Launchpad designed by Novation, in partnership with software developer Ableton, and the first line of physical interfaces from Native Instruments are emblematic of that era.

Novation Launchpad surface control (2009)

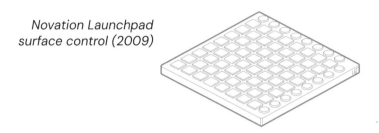

True to their mission, these dedicated interfaces, by their very limitations, were offering higher quality interactions than their predecessors and ensuring the user's time would mostly be spent on *actually* making music. This is a great illustration of the benefits of designing physical and graphical user interfaces together, from the ground up. Besides, on each evolution, new features would appear to reinforce this positioning, for instance, integrated displays to move feedback away from the computer's monitor.

Logically, musicians soon wondered if they could get rid of the computer altogether.

Thanks to the ever decreasing cost of processing power, from the late 2010s, music interfaces started to feature their own DAW running on a computer chip integrated in the interface body itself. In addition to that, autonomous physical machines such as synthesisers, sequencers and samplers, for which general interest had decreased in the 1990s, had come back with fun and innovative interfaces blending the interaction quality of their predecessors

Left: *Native Instruments Maschine MKIII (2017)*

with the possibilities offered by digital synthesis and sampling, all in a much reduced form factor. The 2011 Teenage Engineering OP-1 is probably one of the most iconic examples of this rebirth of machines, openly designed with limitations to induce more creativity in the experience of music making.

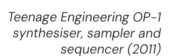
Teenage Engineering OP-1 synthesiser, sampler and sequencer (2011)

Today, the computer DAW has not disappeared and is still very much in use, including for professional recording, arranging and mixing. However, most interfaces and instruments can function without it. Smartphones and tablets have also entered the music-making landscape, and many DAW applications are used on the go with touch-based interactions and haptic feedback that make purely digital workflows much more engaging than they were at the turn of the millennium. In the end, a modern music making studio probably looks more like it did in 1982 than in 2002.

This story, with its many twists and turns, illustrates the deep consequences that interface design decisions can have. It also shows that common assumptions may prove wrong in specific contexts. For instance, when confronted with a new technology, or interface, so versatile that it could technically do anything, it is tempting to deem it the 'ultimate interface' and consider all its predecessors obsolete.

However, by doing so we might overlook the fact that users are not solely concerned with the destination, but also with the journey.

In the case of music making, there have certainly been many positive aspects to the digitisation of the workflow, namely accessibility and creative freedom, to only name a few. However, the almost disappearance of tangible interfaces inherited from traditional and electronic instruments was likely a step too far, and it took many iterations, with sometimes industry-wide pivots, to reach the fine balance we have today, where instruments can take the best from the hardware and software worlds, both in their components and in their interfaces.

'users are not solely concerned with the destination, but also with the journey.'

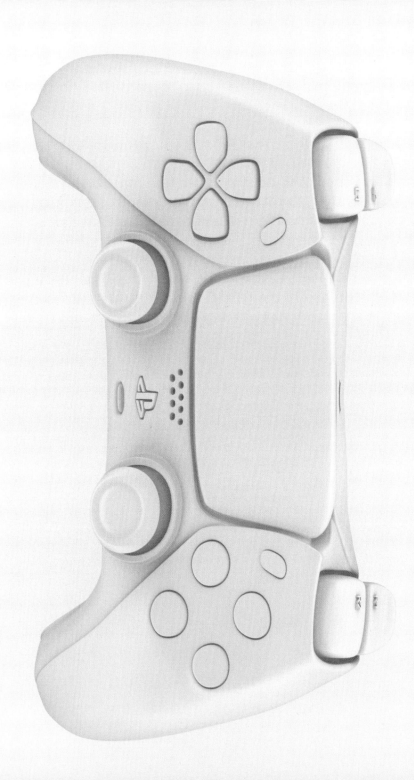

Gamepads

1962's *Spacewar!* is considered the first video game to have made use of a gamepad, that is, a physical interface for a digital game application. First of its kind, it featured two double-throw switches for moving the on-screen spaceship, plus an action button for launching virtual torpedoes. Although its wooden material and cubic form only vaguely suggests its function, it is interesting to note that it already incorporated the core features of a modern gamepad, that is, a (split) directional pad together with an action button.

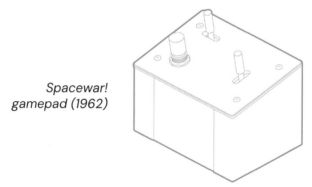

Spacewar!
gamepad (1962)

The first notable design evolution came in 1972 with the Magnavox Odyssey and Atari 2600 Paddle controllers which removed the two switch inputs from their predecessor to feature two knobs instead. Besides giving them the look of portable radios, this meant they could provide more gradual control to the player, since a knob can return continuous values instead of the discrete states returned by a switch.

Left: *Sony Playstation 5 gamepad (2020)*

That change made for the perfect interface to play *Pong*, which would enter history as the first commercially successful video game. Interestingly, *Pong* only required the use of one of the knobs, and would hence enable two players to operate one gamepad simultaneously (although, despite sharing one cable, the Atari 2600 Paddle controller was designed in two parts that could be held separately).

Atari 2600 Paddle controllers (1972)

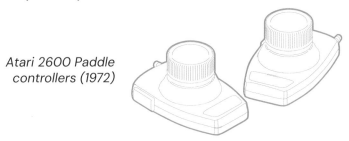

While it was now a time of creative exploration in gamepad design, the late 1970s and early 1980s saw the consolidation of the handheld joystick as the most popular form factor. From an interface perspective, the joystick input came as a logical replacement for the two knobs with which it shared similar properties, while enabling single-handed operations. One hand would now be free to take care of … more action buttons.

Atari CX40 joystick (1977)

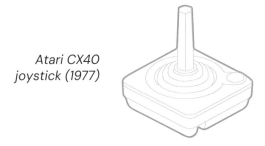

Soon after, however, the first backtracking happened with what would set the gamepad design direction for a long period of time. In 1983, Nintendo released the Nintendo Entertainment System with its gamepad that would become probably the most iconic of all. Allegedly for durability reasons, it featured no joystick or other input capable of returning continuous values. Instead, it introduced the cross shaped directional pad, essentially four buttons bundled together to allow for locomotion in 4 directions.

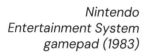
Nintendo Entertainment System gamepad (1983)

The success of this simplified interface in a reduced package influenced the design of the majority of the competing systems for years to come, including the 1994 Sony PlayStation gamepad which, despite its modern ergonomic shape, was in some ways more rudimentary than the 1972 Magnavox Odyssey and Atari 2600 Paddle controllers.

Sony PlayStation gamepad (1994)

In the end, it was not until 1996, and the launch of the Nintendo 64, that continuous value inputs made their comeback on the major interfaces, now in the form of a small joystick (thumb stick).

Nintendo 64
gamepad (1996)

Over the years, new continuous inputs such as triggers were added and, at the turn of the millennium, the architecture of the most popular gamepads evolved to see simple buttons replaced by pressure buttons (capable of returning continuous values) in a quest to always offer more granularity of control to the player. This led to yet another backtracking and, by 2013, all the main gamepads were using simple buttons instead of the theoretically superior pressure ones. In the case of the Sony DualShock 4 gamepad, the sudden disappearance of the face pressure buttons, which had been present since the DualShock 2 version, regularly comes back in video-game forum discussions. However, the vast majority of gamers did not even notice this change at the time, which serves an illustration of the fact that more is not always better when it comes to interfaces.

Over the years, gamepads have become more ergonomic and most are now equipped with motion tracking inputs. In the case of virtual reality, the split interface (one controller in each hand) seems to be the preferred design route, which is somewhat reminiscent of the 1972 Atari 2600 Paddle design, albeit for different reasons. While it would be difficult to argue against the fact that the evolution of game consoles is tightly connected to technological progress, the sometimes surprising paradigm changes in the design of their interfaces highlight interesting design questions.

Meta Quest 2 motion controllers (2020)

Fundamentally, it shows that the quality of an interface is not necessarily the sum of its technical properties. In the two examples of industry-wide design 'U-turns', less advanced inputs were favoured to be more in line with the needs of the players. Of course, this could only have been discovered through incremental modifications following, or leading to, the emergence of popular types of gameplay.

In that sense, it reminds us of the prevalence of the interaction design double interrogation: what does the machine do and how do we, humans, control that? Answering such questions was made significantly harder in a market where the predominant model was evolving to have game console manufacturers on one side and third party game developers on the other (with some exceptions).

Actually, observing the divergent evolution of computer gaming versus console gaming brings another set of interesting insights about interfaces. Indeed, as the mouse and keyboard were taking over on personal computers (PC's), which were primarily intended to be productivity tools, gameplay gained popularity on these machines. Logically, this would allow for making use of complex graphical user interfaces and the finer control provided by a mouse in games too.

This is why, for a long time, menu-heavy war strategy games and first-person shooters were mostly played on PC's, while game consoles would be preferred for the action gameplay of platform games, car racing or sport simulation. Today, the lines are somewhat blurred, since game consoles are capable of providing finer control, and gamepads are commonly used on PC's too.

As for portable gaming, it followed yet another course starting with the Nintendo Game Boy, then becoming almost exclusively a smartphone feature before bouncing back with dedicated portable consoles. In the end, in the short history of interaction design, gamepads remain one of the few examples of a physical interface design allowing for operating a purely digital application directly, that is without the express need for a graphical user interface as a bridge (except for the menus).

Right: Spacewar! gamepad (1962)

7/ The Future of Interfaces

Since the first treatises on architecture, designers have been concerned with the relationship between humans and technology. Understanding materials and construction techniques allowed us to build houses, cities and societies. Machines were invented to help in that process, and to other ends too. Today, interaction design looks specifically at how we interact with them. The detailed stories of the previous chapter all show how humans adapt to, and adopt, technological progress. By examining the combined effects of deep design trends such as 'natural' interactions and disruptive technology changes, including the spread of artificial intelligence, we can paint a picture of the possible future of interface design.

While the three themes are considered independently to avoid unnecessary repetition in the narration, interactions between them are to be expected in the real world.

Artificial intelligence and interfaces

The development of artificial intelligence (AI) sparks fierce debate between those who see it as an opportunity and those who see it as a danger. The future of human activity, and our replacement by AI, is amongst the most pressing questions. However, more than just a technological matter, it also concerns design and, specifically, *interface* design. Of course, this is true of most technology but the unique qualities of AI, including its ability to create, a characteristic long associated with humanity only, might lead us to question our raison d'être, especially in a context where we are easily blinded by our appetite for entertainment.

'It's not the technology, it's how we use it' is a popular catch-all answer which resurfaces in the public space when problems, thought to be arising from technological change, are discussed. Paradoxically, it is as likely to emanate from partisans of fully deregulated technological development as from psychology writers, who encourage a reasonable use of new technologies. While the former simply want to dismiss concerns and keep what they see as a freedom to innovate, the latter seek to protect individuals from technological threats, such as the waste of their attention on meaningless activities. Interestingly, both seem to agree that the responsibility falls on potential users, ignoring what stands between 'technology' and 'how [they] use it'. This, precisely, is the interface. Yet, at each twist and turn of the history of product adoption, we find interface design decisions: the mouse and the graphical user interface made the personal computer, the touchscreen enabled phones to become 'smart' and, without voice interfaces, there would

> *'Technology, on its own, is neutral; the design of interfaces is not.'*

be no digital assistant on kitchen worktops. Sometimes, interfaces are designed against the user's interest — on purpose. This is typically the case of websites and mobile applications that use 'deceptive patterns' to trick individuals into adopting behaviours they did not mean to adopt. Technology, on its own, is neutral; the design of interfaces is not.

The effect of AI on human activity cannot be fully examined without considering the evolution of human-machine collaboration and the hard truth that comes with it: at some point, AI might not need us anymore. Until recently, machines were merely amplifying human natural abilities. Even the most advanced automations would need a clear instruction from the user in order to return a result. For instance, an illustrator using a traditional graphic design application would need to use a combination of their experience, time and skills to produce an interesting logo. To use a mathematical metaphor, machines could only *multiply* what the user would provide. Generative AI changed that and enabled machines to massively extend an individual's natural abilities. A similar logo can now be generated instantly, without any skill or experience. Machines can still multiply, and now they can *add* too. In the history of technological development, the design of interfaces was made all the more important because humans played a central role in human–machine collaboration. If we keep the same utilitarian approach, it might limit how we think

about future interfaces, for humans seem to become the inessential party in this collaboration. Before we know it, we might be considering interface design, not as the way we use technology but as the way technology uses us.

Etymologically, 'design' shares roots with 'intent'. Clarifying our intentions with AI will help us design interactions that correspond to human, rather than machine, needs. But prioritising human needs requires making choices too. For instance, it seems that AI could help us learn faster, get better at what we do and achieve our goals. Alternatively, it could also take care of the various tasks around us while we indulge in leisure activities. Of course, it's tempting to see this as an individual choice, and it might indeed be — to some extent. However, there is a difference between building interactions that encourage the creation of original work, art and ideas, and interactions aimed at frictionless consumption. Let's consider the 'creative' industry. If we choose frictionless consumption, the idea that a few humans keep creating for the rest of humanity, using AI, seems unrealistic.

'Before we know it, we might be considering interface design, not as the way we use technology but as the way technology uses us.'

The need for 'creatives', effectively creation operators, will likely disappear, the same way computer operators disappeared when computers became personal. More likely, consumers would become their own creation operators, having their desires communicated to machines, as content is being generated, on the fly, to match their exact taste. While this might sound exaggerated, it is not very far off from the way AI interfaces have been designed so far. What is the assembly of text 'prompts' but the expression of desires in a language best suited to the way AI functions? While it can involve a level of creative thinking, it is a massive oversimplification of what the creative process is. Creation is not purely result driven. Creation involves abstract thinking and exploration. In 1967, French philosopher Guy Debord analysed the global shift toward a society driven by consumption as entertainment [1]. His argument revolved around the idea that our obsession with commodities and image turned authentic life into its representation, and consumption into consumerism. As we seem to be rising to a new paradigm that we could call 'creation as entertainment', the daunting hypothesis of humans giving up true creation, and, in a similar fashion, other fields of human activity, cannot be ignored.

In this context, what prevents us from designing interfaces for AI using a wider palette of inputs and new conceptual models that encourage exploration, abstract thinking and more diverse forms of expression?

It is established that AI will sooner or later be part of most machines and will be used for most applications, creative or not. Whether it represents a danger or an opportunity for human activity is largely a question of interface, as is the case with most technological change.

Ironically, AI might soon not need humans anymore, which will force us to rethink the role of interface design in a less utilitarian, and more human, way. Ultimately, the question of which interactions we design, and to what end, cannot be eluded, for it will most certainly influence the role AI plays in society.

'As we seem to be rising to a new paradigm that we could call "creation as entertainment", the daunting hypothesis of humans giving up true creation, and, in a similar fashion, other fields of human activity, cannot be ignored.'

What future for UX and UI design?

The histories of computers and software applications are tightly intertwined. In most cases, applications remain the base unit to describe the different uses a computer can have. From the user's perspective, this is a well understood conceptual model which has successfully spread to other machines. The rise of the smartphone, with millions of mobile applications, or 'apps', has driven the growth of user experience (UX) and user interface (UI) as popular fields of design. However, the application model might be limiting how we build the future of computing and how we design interactions with everything else. In parallel, artificial intelligence will drastically change the way we think about software development. If the omnipresent application disappears, it will have a profound effect on UX and UI design as we know it.

Spatial computing is an umbrella concept that covers all the immersive technologies and their interfaces, including headsets and glasses that bring virtual content directly to the user's eye. From a technical standpoint, adapting the application model to spatial computing seems like a reasonable idea; from a business perspective, a great one. For the user, however, it might come at a disadvantage. In the mid 2010s, virtual reality (VR) started to become popular and, today, each VR application has its own environment inside which the user is teleported upon launch. Conceptually, it makes sense, for immersion is a sought-after feature of virtual reality. With the growth of spatial computing and, for use cases that go beyond entertainment, jumping from one virtual world to the next, with each application, might not be as desirable.

'In real life, a pencil, a pair of scissors and a stick of glue can be used together without having to move into a separate workshop corresponding to each — even if they come from three different suppliers.'

Typically where the user's environment is meant to play a role, it is the virtual elements that should integrate, seamlessly, into their physical reality. Yet, with the application model in its current form, users find themselves having to choose between immersive 'full-screen' experiences, where their physical reality is replaced — or altered — and 'windowed' experiences, restricted to a limited part of their field of view. In both cases, the implementation works against the seamless integration of virtual elements into their physical reality. Alternatively, an invisible implementation of applications may be favoured, for instance with a hidden graphical user interface. In that case, however, users are likely to be confused as to which application they are using, and why interactions sometimes change, when everything else remains apparently the same. Moving to a conceptual model centred around tools might be a better alternative. In real life, a pencil, a pair of scissors and a stick of glue can be used together without having to move into a separate workshop corresponding to each — even if they come from three different suppliers. Similarly, users would be right to expect to be able to use tools from different developers simultaneously, like widgets. In that scenario, there would be no notion of switching applications, let alone exporting files, although it would imply technical challenges such as rethinking file standards and sharing technologies that are often proprietary. Moreover, without the menu structure imposed by applications, wireframes, user journeys and graphical user interfaces would probably need to be rethought to be able to accommodate user needs dynamically, and contextually.

In 2009, Apple started using 'There's an app for that' in television advertisements to demonstrate the wide range of possible use cases an iPhone could have. At the time, approximately 170 million smartphones were sold per year globally. By 2016, this figure had almost been multiplied by 10 for an estimated 2.5 billion users in the world. Easy to carry and intuitive to use, the smartphone has truly become the personal computer — and much more. By doing so, it has gradually replaced a wide array of devices and their users have lost the diversity of interactions they were used to: 'There's an app for that' is a stronger argument when one already has a smartphone in their pocket. In response, a growing number of users are now looking to reconnect with more traditional devices, which provide enhanced kinaesthetic experiences. The enthusiasm for manual photography, modular synthesisers and record turntables illustrates this phenomenon and echoes a deeper trend of individuals trying to move away from their screen. History will tell if spatial computing is perceived as a solution, or an aggravation, to this issue, and it might very well come down to the technology used to display virtual content into human eyes. However, the way we design future interfaces and interactions will, undoubtedly, have an influence on that matter too. Even if computing is to be fully dematerialised, there is a good chance that users will still want to anchor some of their activities into tangible interactions. In that sense, giant graphical user interfaces that float in the air should, probably, not be seen as a means, and end, to every single future human activity. Instead, UX and UI designers could start exploring how they can augment the physical interfaces that users already love, and build new ones that take the best of the physical and the digital worlds.

With the rise of language inputs and voice assistants powered by AI it is increasingly unlikely that users will want to stick to the segregation of tasks imposed by applications. In a 2023 Reddit post named 'AI is About to Completely Change How You Use Computers', Microsoft co-founder Bill Gates suggested that applications will soon be replaced by artificial intelligence in the form of what he calls 'agents'. As a direct reference to the popularisation of the graphical user interface in the 1980s, in which he participated, he announces the 'biggest revolution in computing since we went from typing commands to tapping on icons'. If we consider what AI is already capable of, we could indeed imagine a situation where not only applications disappear, but their developers too. In concrete terms, there would be no more programs, functions or lines of code written by humans. Instead, functionalities would likely be generated instantaneously, based on each user's demand and ability to describe their need. From an interaction standpoint, it does not necessarily mean that language would remain the only input. On the contrary, new inputs, new interaction modalities and even new typologies of feedback could be formed spontaneously, with any object potentially becoming the most extravagant interface. A sofa could be turned into an electronic bagpipe; a wooden stick into a 3D sculpting tool; and a dining table into a giant gamepad, with each plate acting as a tangible input to control a game projected spatially. Of course, this is all speculative and if this was, indeed, to become technically feasible, there would be no more UX and UI designers than there would be developers. In that sense it connects more generally to the question of what we want to do with AI explored above.

From antique architecture to interactions, the way we design is always concerned with the evolution of society at large. UX and UI design have grown into highly popular fields of design with the rise of the mobile application as the front end of most new products and services. Yet, the spatialisation of computing and the evolution of user expectations might prompt a change in how we perceive what applications can do for us. Artificial intelligence might even replace applications, and the people who create them. Ultimately, this could affect the way we design everything.

'new inputs, new interaction modalities and even new typologies of feedback could be formed spontaneously, with any object potentially becoming the most extravagant interface.'

The end of interactions

We seem to be on the verge of witnessing the biggest change in the history of human–machine interactions. While our pursuit of making technology disappear will probably result in bringing it inside the human brain, our love for automation and the irresistible attraction power of artificial intelligence might take us to a new stage in the human–machine relationship: the age of prediction.

In 1992, American political scientist Francis Fukuyama declared we had reached 'the end of history', the moment where humanity would stabilise into one uniform political system, rendering the idea of evolution obsolete[2]. Fukuyama saw Western democracy as the final form of human organisation, and the collapse of the Eastern Bloc seemed to prove him right. Similarly, technological breakthroughs increasingly result in reasoning to promote the idea that we are on the threshold of technological singularity.

In the world of interface design, making interactions feel 'natural' is certainly a popular idea that encourages the use of the body over physical proxies. In that respect, gestures, touch and voice interactions all seem to share the same ambition: make technology disappear and turn the body into the interface. In practice, they often rely extensively on graphical user interfaces and lack the tangibility of traditional interfaces, which limits their use. This is why some see body implants, and especially the brain–computer interface, as the last frontier, the ultimate interface that will replace all the others and, de facto, mark the end of interface history.

If we accept that (i) human thoughts could be one day fully decoded — and encoded — and that (ii) humans would be willing, and allowed, to have interfaces implanted into their brain for purposes other than medical ones, then we could imagine that a lot of our daily interactions with machines would go through that channel. Driving a car, playing a video game or even writing a message would be as 'simple' an interaction as emitting a thought. This raises multiple questions, for thoughts are not exactly simple to control. However, some believe that this is the only way to allow for the true expression of human capability, powered by abstract intellectual processes only. According to that vision, today's interfaces do not enable expression but, much to the contrary, restrict it, by making it dependent on other factors such as acquired skills and complex interactions.

Of course, the exact opposite set of arguments can be formed. In *Creative and Mental Growth*, often considered one of the most influential art education textbooks, Viktor Lowenfeld and W. Lambert Brittain propose that varied experiences of interaction are — precisely — what allows for abstract intellectual processes, and enables human expression[3]. As often, the truth may be somewhere in between, depending on people and precise use cases. But what if, along with what already looks like a radical shift of paradigm, something more fundamental changes? *What if the disappearance of interfaces leads to the disappearance of the notion of intentionality too?*

At the turn of the 2010s, tracking and sensors emerged as a complement, and sometimes replacement, for more traditional inputs such as touchscreens, buttons and knobs. Where the latter would rely exclusively on active interaction mechanisms, the former would allow for both active and passive interactions. A microphone, for instance, can activate a light switch based on verbal instructions from the user ('switch on the light'), or by inferring that the user arrived home through sound wave analysis.

Until recently, passive interactions have mostly relied on rule-based systems with limited complexity and exposed parameters to offer a degree of user control. Usually referred to as 'automation', a typical use case would be to simplify interactions with home appliances. With implantable brain-computer interfaces, the amount of parameters to take into account makes it unlikely that such interactions would still rely on simple rule-based systems. Most likely, artificial intelligence, already tasked with the encoding and decoding of neural information, would also be used for what it is great at: prediction. And specifically, *the prediction of our intentions*. Lights could turn on just as we feel it is getting dark, messages of apologies sent as we remember an invitation letter left unopened, food ordered as we look at a banana on the kitchen table.

'What if the disappearance of interfaces leads to the disappearance of the notion of intentionality too?'

This raises questions about how to signal the possible interactions and how to provide feedback when they occur. But can we still speak of 'interaction' if machine response is triggered before the intention is fully formed in the human brain? In fact, would there be any way for someone to know if an intention was about to be formed, once they witness, and hence become influenced by, machine response? And what about more complex human–machine interactions? Would people be able to discriminate between original thoughts and those, subcontracted to a machine, fed back to them as the most natural intuitions?

This book started with a short timeline of interface history, which, until now, has also been the history of our interactions with machines. If prediction replaces interaction, the very notion of interface might disappear and, along with it, the distinction between humans and machines.

'can we still speak of "interaction" if machine response is triggered before the intention is fully formed in the human brain?'

'If prediction replaces interaction, the very notion of interface might disappear and, along with it, the distinction between humans and machines.'

1: Guy Debord, La Société du Spectacle (Buchet–Chastel, 1967).

2: Francis Fukuyama, The End of History and the Last Man (Free Press, 1992).

3: Viktor Lowenfeld and W. Lambert Brittain, Creative and Mental Growth (Macmillan Publishing Company, 1987), page 6.

Acknowledgments

We would like to give a huge thanks to Harm van Kessel and Peter Notebaart at BIS who made this book possible.

We would also like to warmly thank our editor Sebastian Rydberg for his great suggestions, Esmeralda Atzamalidou for her help in putting this book together and Kate Crossland-Page for her meticulous proofreading.

Finally, this book would not have been the same without the acute feedback from Alice McGurran, Arthur Carabott, Ashley Wiltshire, Benton Ching, Giulio Ammendola, Govind Balakrishnan, Henri Peugeot, Hubert Mathias, Julian Melchiorri, Léonard Heuse, Luke David Harris, Marek Bereza, Markus Lahtinen, Michael Moran, Nicolas Gavard, Rodrigo García González, Samya Mathias, Sanya Rai Gutpa, Timi Oyedeji, Vitaliy Tyzhnevyy and Yuki Machida.

Biographies

Guillaume Couche

Guillaume Couche is the co-founder of Wolf in Motion, ranked #1 design agency for User Experience in the iF World Design Index 2021. His work has been featured by Time, BBC, Wired, Dezeen and FastCo and he is the recipient of multiple design awards including Lexus, Core77, and iF. He has been a visiting lecturer at the Royal College of Art, Imperial College London, and Lund University since 2015.

Richard Shackleton

Richard Shackleton is a Partner at Wolf in Motion. Starting with an MEng Degree in Software Engineering at Imperial College London he has 30 years of experience leading strategy, innovation and product design at creative technology companies. He is an early stage investor and strategic advisor to multiple successful design and creative business founders.

Samuel Iliffe

Samuel Iliffe is a Designer at Wolf In Motion and former Design Researcher in Residence at the Design Museum London. Following a BEng Degree in Mechanical Engineering from Queen Mary University of London he completed a double Masters Degree in Innovation Design Engineering at the Royal College of Art and Imperial College London.